RISE OF WORLD ANTHROPOLOGY

About the Author

LALITA PRASAD VIDYARTHI (b. 1931) received his doctorate from the University of Chicago and is now Professor and Chairman of the Department of Anthropology at the University of Ranchi, India. Currently (1974-1978) he is the President of the International Union of Anthropological and Ethnological Sciences and of the 10th International Congress of Anthropological and Ethnological Sciences to be held in India in 1978. Dr. Vidyarthi is the President of the Indian Anthropological Association, a Founder-Member of the Indian Council of Social Sciences Research, Chairman of the Task Force on Development of Tribal Areas of the Planning Commission, and a Member of the Central Council on Tribal Research Institute of the Ministry of Home Affairs, Government of India. He is Founder-Editor of The Journal of Social Research, The Indian Anthropologist, and The Research Journal of Ranchi University. His major fields of research are the Tribal Culture of India including the Andaman and Nicobar Islands; Urban-Industrial political, and action Anthropology; Indian Civilization, the History of Indian Culture, Folklore, village studies and History of Anthropological Theories.

He has to his credit several internationally popular books.

RISE OF WORLD ANTHROPOLOGY

As Reflected through the International Congresses, 1934—1978

L.P. Vidyarthi

CONCEPT PUBLISHING COMPANY PVT. LTD.
NEW DELHI-110059

ISBN : 978-93-88937-35-1

Edition 2020

Published and Printed by

Concept
Since 1974

Concept Publishing Company Pvt. Ltd.
A/15-16, Commercial Block, Mohan Garden,
New Delhi-110059 (INDIA)
T : +91 11 25351460, +91 11 25351794
E : publishing@conceptpub.com, *W* : www.conceptpub.com

Contents

List of Plates

Preface

Anthropology has been on march through the ages. The 'Child of Darwin' as Marret called it, in a way, celebrated its centenary with *The Origin of Species* in 1859. It took however, a considerably long time to get it professionally institutionalized on the global plane when the British anthropologists took the initiative to organize the First International Congress of Anthropological and Ethnological Sciences (ICAES) in London in 1934. By this time, the British evolutionary and diffusionist theories had already sustained a setback and the British structural-functional school had emerged as the most important school. This formative phase of institutionalization of Anthropology further strengthened the British Social Anthropology, and created a climate in its favour on the global level. This trend was further entrenched during the Second World Congress held at Copenhagen in 1938. During the second world war, Anthropology, however, became almost dead and needed a revitalisation.

When the Congress met in Vienna in 1952, with Wilhelm Schmidt, the noted scholar of Austrian school of diffusion, the 'Science of Man', as it were, was reborn after the ravages of the second world war. With increased vigour, it covered new areas of research, and thus created a climate for consolidation and expansion. The World Congress held in Philadelphia (1956), for the first time in the United States, amply brought to light the post-war dominance of American Anthropology. It was marked by participation of scholars drawn from different parts of the world including the delegates from the USSR, for the first time. The Philadelphia Congress viewed in the background of historic International Symposium on Anthropology organised by Wenner-Gren Foundation for Anthropological Research at New York in 1952 under the chairmanship of A.L. Kroeber accelerated support to the American model of Anthropology. In his introductory remarks, Kroeber observes emphatically :

> After all, the subject of Anthropology is limited only by man. It is not restricted by time, it goes back into geology as far as men can be traced. It is not restricted by region but it is world-wide in scope. It has specialised on the primitives because no other science would deal seriously with them, it has never renounced its intent to understand the higher civilisations also.
>
> (A.L. KROEBER : 1953 : XIII)

This American model of Anthropology decidedly found all round recognition in the symposium and, among many, Levi-Strauss agreed that "Anthropology has a close relationship with the Humanities, the Social Sciences and the natural sciences." He further observed : "Anthropology tries to jump to a deep level, while Social Sciences have been, so far, unable to do so, and the result is an extremely difficult situation for cooperation between Anthropology and the Social Sciences (Sociology)."

(1953 : 154)

In the course of the discussion, Margaret Mead, whose demise recently has taken away a great scholar from the field of World Anthropology, further clarified Levi-Strauss's stand and amplified his statement. She observes :

> Anthropology uses methods of analysis from different levels (Embryology, Geology) with different units and different time scales, cross-cutting all disciplines relating man to nature, on the one hand, and in History, on the other, while Sociology is an analysis on a single level, leaving psychological and biological analysis to other disciplines.
>
> (M. MEAD : 1953 : 154)

The integrated image of Anthropology, which emerged from the 1952 symposium and its approaches for studying the 'integrated' man, was further followed up in the planning and deliberation of the Fifth International Congress of Anthropological and Ethnological Sciences (1956) as well as in the publication of the book entitled *Current Anthropology* (William Thomas : 1956). The American Anthropology, further enriched itself by initiating the publication of *Current Anthropology*, a world journal of the 'Science of Man', edited by Sol Tax since 1960. It carried the spirit of integration further in Anthropology as it continued to publish papers from all over the world on "Prehistory, Archaeology, Linguistics, Folklore, Ethnology, Social Anthropology and Physical Anthropology."

(TAX : 1960)

Such an approach continued to dominate the international scene, and even in the Paris Congress (1960), where structural-functional school was deeply entrenched, the American model of Anthropology found better projection.

A ground, however, for richer mix was under preparation and when the Congresses met in Moscow (1964), Tokyo-Kyoto (1968) and Chicago (1973), they evidently reflected better interactions of man and minds of ideas, concepts and theories. The Soviet Ethnography developed on the lines of evolutionary theory and further modified by the writings of Marx, Engels and Lenin, marked the revival of a new dimension in Anthropology, and made it more balanced, and somewhat free from Anglo-American influences. Referring to the recognition of such a trend in Anthropology, a Soviet ethnographer, Y.V. Averkiyeva observes :

> Beginning with the 1950s, we observe a feverish search for a 'theory of development' in fact, even an 'Anthropology of development' emerged. By the end of 1950 this search took the form of 'renaissance of evolutionism', vividly expressed in connection with the centenary of the publication of Darwin's *The Origin of Species* when, as Julian Steward, the well-known US anthropologist, described it, there was a 'universial proclamation' of evolutionism.

(AVERKIYEVA : 1974 : 312)

Marvin Harris terms this approach as neo-cultural materialism which is a sort of synthesis of the ideas of neo-evolutionism and improved Marxism.

(MARVIN HARRIS : 1968)

Such a revival, reinterpretation and recognition of neo-evolutionism to understand class societies is a significant development in the contemporary anthropological theories and is a pointer to a greater mix and expanding horizon of Anthropology. The Tokyo (1968) and the Chicago (1973) Congresses were also planned from the beginning to include as many scholars from every part of the world as possible. Such a planning and execution ensured better interaction among scholars and a balanced internationalization of the 'Science of Man'.

Anthropology, however, continues to be a product of the European-American traditions. So far, the Congress was neither held in a Third World Country nor the scholars of the 'most-researched countries' were allowed to play their rightful roles. All these led to the growth of the concept of Colonial Anthropology or neo-imperialism in Anthropology. Jan J. Loubser, for example, expresses concern for " 'the existing vertical' relationship between social scientists in Europe and North America and then in the Third World which implies, though not explicitly, intellectual imperialism and colonial exploitation."

(JAN J. LOUBSER : 1977)

Such nations are likely to decline, if the scholars from the Third World countries are allowed to play their due roles. The Tenth International Congress of Anthropological and Ethnological Sciences, which is being held, for the first time, in a Third World country, is a pointer towards the Anthropology for the future.

Thus, during the past 44 years, in the nine Congresses held at London (1934), Copenhagen (1938), Brussels (1948), Vienna (1952), Philadelphia (1956), Paris (1960), Moscow (1964), Tokyo (1968), and Chicago (1973), more than 4,700 papers were presented on various aspects of anthropological sciences. As the Congress got more and more internationalised, the number of participating countries, scholars and papers went on increasing. In the first Congress, only 290 papers were presented but in the last Congress (1973) the number of papers increased to 2,000.

As a part of the International Union of Anthropological and Ethnological Sciences (IUAES) programme as well as my presidential endeavour, I collected as much relevant materials as possible to assess the varied types of developments in the fields of Anthropology as reflected through these Congresses.

From my communication with Prof. Lawrence Krader, Secretary-General, I learn that a similar proposal was mooted in 1966, as a result of which a short note, highlighting some basic information about the former Congresses, was circulated at the Chicago Congress (1973).

In my capacity as the tenth President of the Congress, I accepted the challenge to write a somewhat broad-based history of the Congress as well as the activities of the IUAES. I visited most of the knowledgeable persons in each of the places and collected information from both primary and secondary sources. I also wrote several personal letters to the concerned colleagues in this connection but the response was not at all encouraging.

While it is not possible to acknowledge the suppo1t and help received from the various institutions and persons individually in completion of the task, I have been specially inspired and encouraged by the kind support received from Dr. Anna Hohenwart who was good enough to provide me the draft on the Congresses held at Brussels, Vienna and Paris. Prof. Lawrence Krader, who has been closely associated with organization of the ICAES and IUAES for quite a long period (1962-1978), has done me a great favour by giving his experiences about this world organisation which is being published without any modification.

I also take this opportunity to thank Mr. William Fagg of British Museum, Prof. Raymond Firth, Prof. C. von Furer-Haimendorf and Prof. Jcnathan Benthal, Director of the Royal Anthropological Institute, London, for their guidance and help, in tracing, especially, the origin of Congress (1934) as well as its evolution.

For the materials on Paris Congress, I am thankful to Dr. Robert Gessain, and for Tokyo-Kyoto Congress to Professors Masao Oka and Chie Nakane, without whose help I would not have been able to complete the chapters on these Congresses.

While preparing this book, my pupil and colleague, Dr. Akhauri Ratish N. Srivastava has been of great help, and it is because of his cooperation that the completion of this work could be possible. Dr. Asesh Haldar and Dr. P. Dash Sharma have extended their ungrudging support in collecting data from the very inception of this project. I am thankful to them for this cooperation.

I am also grateful to Dr. Vinayshil Gautam as he could supervise its production and made it ready for distribution in the Congress (1978). Mr. Ramautar Prasad has provided all the secretarial assistance. Sri Naurang Rai has taken personal interest in its production. I am thankful to them for their hard work and active cooperation.

I will consider my efforts amply rewarded, if this small work of mine is of some help to our colleauges in understanding the chief features of the World Congresses in particular, and of the evolution of Anthropology in general, reflected through the scientific and other related activities of the ICAES and IUAES.

L.P. VIDYARTHI

REFERENCES

Averkiyeva, Y.P. 1974 : "Neo-Evolutionism, Relativism and Racialism" in *Races and People : Contemporary Ethnic and Racial Problems*, I.R. Grigulevich and S.V. Kozlov (*eds.*) Moscow, Progress Publishers, pp. 308-320.

Darwin, Charles 1859 : *The Origin of Species*, New York, The New American Library of World Literature Inc. (Mentor Edition : 1958).

Harris, Marvin 1968 : *The Rise of Anthropological Theory*, London, Routledge and Kegan Paul.

Kroeber, A.L. 1953 : *Anthropology Today* : An Encyclopaedic Inventory (ed.), Chicago, Illinois, The University of Chicago Press.

Levi-Strauss, C. 1953 : On "Problems of Process : Theory" in Sol Tax *et. al.* (ed.) *An Appraisal of Anthropology Today*, Chicago, The University of Chicago Press. p.154.

Loubser, Jan, J. 1977 : The Need for the Indigenization of the Social Sciences. Paper presented at the General Conference of the National Councils and Analogous Bodies, ISSC, UNESCO, October 24-26, Paris.

Mead, M. 1953 : On "Problems of Process : Theoty" in Sol Tax *et. al.* (ed.) *An Appraisal of Anthropology Today*, Chicago, The University of Chicago Press, p.154.

Tax, Sol 1960 : *Current Anthropology*, vol. 1, No. 1.

Thomas, Jr. William L. (ed.) 1956 : *Current Anthropology* : A Supplement to *Anthropology Today*, Chicago, The University of Chicago Press.

PART ONE

INSTITUTIONALISATION : THE EARLY PHASE

1

The London Congress : 1934

The First International Congress of Anthropological and Ethnological Sciences

I. THE BACKGROUND

As was noted in the preceding introductory chapter, the International Congress of Anthropological and Ethnological Sciences (ICAES) was founded in 1934 on the initiative of a few anthropologists-ethnologists who held their first Congress in London in July 1934. According to the Abstract volume on *Congress International Des Sciences Anthropologiques et Etanologiques* released on the occasion of the first ICAES, more than 900 anthropologists, ethnologists and scientists of allied fields from 43 countries participated in the Conference. The following is the break ups of the institutions which participated in the London Congress :

1.	Universities	67
2.	Governments	57
3.	Academic Societies	144

From among these three sets of institutions a Britain-based organising committee was constituted. It had the following as its members :

1. His Grace the Archbishop of Canterbury.
2. His Grace the Duke of Abercorn.
3. Right Hon. the Lord Mayor of London.
4. Sir Charles Close, President, International Population Congress.
5. Field Marshal Sir William Birdwood, Master of Peterhouse, Cambridge.
6. The Right Hon. S.M. Bruce, High Commissioner for Australia.
7. Maj.-General Sir Percy Z. Cox, President, Royal Geographical Society.
8. The Hon. G.H. Ferguson, High Commissioner for Canada.
9. Sir James G. Frazer.
10. Admiral Sir W.E. Goodenough, former President, Royal Geographical Society.
11. Sir George F. Hill, Director, British Museum.
12. Prof. T.C. Hodson, Professor of Social Anthropology, Cambridge.
13. Rev. Prof. E.O. James, University of Leeds.
14. Sir Arthur Keith, Master of the Buckston Browne Research Farm, Downe.
15. The Lord Lugard, President, International Institute of African Languages and Cultures.
16. Sir Edward D. Maclagan, President, Royal Asiatic Society.
17. Dr. R.R. Marett, Reader in Social Anthropology, Oxford.
18. Dr. Allan Mawer, Provost of University College, London.
19. Sir Bhupendra Nath Mitra, High Commissioner for India.
20. Hon. Sir James Parr, High Commissioner for New Zealand.
21. Sir Charles Peers, President, Society of Antiquaries of London.

22. Prof. Sir Flinders Petrie, University College, London.
23. The Lord Raglan, Former President, Anthropological Section, British Association.
24. Sir Humphery Rolleston, President, Eugenics Society.
25. Professor H.J. Rose, President, Folklore Society.
26. Sir E. Denison Rose, Director, School of Oriental Studies.
27. Rev. E.W. Smith, President, Royal Anthropological Institute.
28. Hon. C. Te Water, High Commissioner for the Union of South Africa.
29. Sir Archibald Weigall, Chairman, Royal Empire Society.
30. Sir Henry S. Wellocome, Curator, Wellcome Historical Medical Museum.
31. The Earl Winterton.
32. The Marquees of Zetland.

In addition to the broad-based committee, a small Executive Committee was nominated. The following were its office-bearers :

Patron : The Duke of York.
President : The Earl of Onslow.
Vice-Presidents : E. Fischer, W. Koppers, P. Rivet, S. Sergi, K. Stolyhwo, Th. Thomsen.
Secretaries : J.L. Myres and A.H. Brodrick.
Treasurer : H.G. Beasley.

The Congress met in London from July 30 to August 4, 1934. It spelled out three main objectives :

(*a*) To review recent advances in knowledge in anthropological and ethnological sciences,
(*b*) To compare experiences and ideas,
(*c*) To add something to the notion of what man is, and what man does.

In short, the central theme of the Congress was 'Man and His Works'.

II. THE CONGRESS IN ACTION

1. The Inauguration

The Congress was inaugurated by the brother of the Duke of York on 30 July 1934. The Earl of Onslow presided over the Congress. In his presidential address, he emphasised on the use of the knowledge of Anthropology in Diplomacy and Colonial Administration in dealing with the races of alien civilization. The Earl remarked :

> In more recent times the tendency has been to encourage native civilization to develop on its own lines and to absorb rather than to initiate European ideas. But the old idea of Europeanization is by no means dead especially as regards methods of government. Take East Africa, for instance. Here, we have a community consisting of Europeans, Asiatics and Africans. The Europeans are mainly of British stock, the Asiatics are Indians and Arabs, the Africans are the native race or rather races, for there are four distinct groups of languages. Can anyone conceive communities more different than these, or differing more essentially from a European country ? It is, I feel sure, impossible to solve the difficulties which such community experiences simply by imposing a copy of European methods . . .

He further observed :

> You cannot bring out the best of a native civilization or develop and improve native culture unless you thoroughly understand it, and this is what anthropology helps you to do. Anthropology is perhaps a new science, and the idea of encouraging its serious study in administrators does not find favour on all hands. It is said that the Anthropologist is 'unpractical' and 'academic'. I think it was Professor Malinowski, who exploded this idea, at any rate as regards the anthropologist of today. He points out in his interesting article on the rationalization of anthropology that anthropologists of a previous generation preferred

> to study 'man dead rather than alive'. It was 'the science of skulls and skeletons of pleistocene or neolithic man' but, the modern anthropologist is of different temper . . .

The Earl of Onslow emphasised the need of training in Anthropology, especially for the administrator. He said :

> It is true of course that a knowledge of anthropology will not make any man a sound practical administrator, any more than profound knowledge of the law will necessarily make a great advocate. Still it cannot be denied that legal knowledge must be of value to an advocate, and in the same way anthropological knowledge must be of value to an administrator. This knowledge will not turn a bad official into a good one, but it will render the task of the good official easier.

2. Special Features

In the inaugural and following day sessions, special invitees were Sir Aurel Stein, Prof. T.C. Hodson, Rev. Prof. R. Marett, and Dr. J.B.S. Haldane. Sir Stein's talk was based on his work done under the auspices of the Archaeological Survey of the Indian Government in 1927-28.

Prof. Hodson of Cambridge University lectured on the aspects of Indian society, on the basis of the information drawn from the Census of India, 1931.

Rev. Prof. Marett talked about the growth and tendency of anthropological and ethnological studies. He outlined the development of anthropology as revealed by its teaching at Oxford, Cambridge and London Universities.

Dr. J.B.S. Haldane, a noted scientist of London University, spoke on Anthropology and human biology. He emphasised on how a biologist can help anthropologists in the field of genetics.

3. Organisation of the Scientific Sessions

A quick survey on the papers as included in the Abstract of the Proceedings of the London Congress leads us to reflect upon the prevailing interests of that period. The anthropological papers were classified as follows :

1.1. Anatomy and Physical Anthropology (55 papers)
1.2. Anthropometry and the Standardization of Techniques (39 papers)
2. Psychology (17 papers)
3. Demography and Population Problems (13 papers)
4.1. Ethnography, General (29 papers)
4.2. Ethnography, Africa (20 papers)
4.3. Ethnography, America (16 papers)
5. Technology (21 papers)
6. Sociology (34 papers)
7. Religion (25 papers)
8. Language and Writing (23 papers).

Except one section, viz., Demography and Population Problem, each of the above sectional meetings was held under the supervision of the person (Chairman) who was assisted by several other persons (Vice-Chairmen) and Secretaries. Further, each of the above mentioned sectional meetings (hereafter termed as session) was held for from two to four days, from July 31 to August 3.

Over 290 papers were read and discussed in as many as 11 sessions. The following are the details of these sessions :

1. Physical Anthropology

Under this broad category two sections were included. These were :

(1) Anatomy, and
(2) Anthropometry.

Altogether, 94 papers were contributed to these sections of Anthropology.

1.1. *Anatomy*

A five-day session on various aspects of Anatomy and

Physical Anthropology was held under the Chairmanship of Prof. Sir Grafton Elliot Smith of London University. The topics of discussions were :

(1) Man's place among the primates (4 papers)
(2) Fossil anthropology (6 papers)
(3) The Growth pattern in children (5 papers)
(4) The Role of the Endocrine Glands in relation to growth and racial differences with special reference to the anterior pituitary (1 paper)
(5) Anthropological aspects of blood grouping (12 papers)
(6) Comparative Anatomy of the brain (5 papers)
(7) The menstural cycle in man and primate in relation to the harmones and behaviour characteristics (4 papers)
(8) Genetics (4 papers)
(9) Aspects of Dentition (2 papers)
(10) The Radiographic depiction of the organ of speech (1 paper)
(11) Growth of the jaws with special reference to the milk dentition and the period of change (4 papers)
(12) The Localization of function in the cerebral cortex (4 papers), and
(13) Bodily habitas (6 papers)

Altogether 58 scholars presented their research findings on various aspects of Anatomy. It is to be noted that out of 58 contributions, 22 were from the various universities of England, five from the U.S.A. and the rest from other parts of Europe and Africa. From Asia only Hong Kong was represented.

1.2. *Anthropometry and Standardization of Techniques*

Another four-day session was held on 'Anthropometry and the Standardization of Techniques' under the Chairmanship of Prof. H.J. Fleure of Manchester University. Six papers were presented on anthropometric measurements, eight papers were on the standardization of techniques, involving the interpretation of Physical Anthropology data.

Included in this session was 'Regional Physical Anthropology' in which the following contributions were presented :

(1) Finland and England (4 contributors)
(2) Asia (6 contributors)
(3) Africa (6 contributors), and
(4) Europe (10 contributors).

2. Psychology

A four-day session was held on Psychology, under the chairmanship of Prof. F.C. Bartelett of Cambridge University. Under this session, 17 papers were read and discussions were held on:

(1) Social Psychology (4 papers)
(2) The contact of cultures (5 papers)
(3) Current theorists in psychology and the social significance of present day trends (8 papers).

The discussion on Social Psychology included development of Social Psychology, field work in Social Psychology (Eastern Asia and New Guinea) and religious and economic sections in a Santu tribe. Except for one, all contributions were from England.

The session on 'The Contact of Culture' included the paper presentation by Prof. Arnold Toynbee of London University, who talked about psychological problems arising from the contact of cultures. This was followed by four papers developed on contact situations.

Six papers were read on the theme of the 'Social Significance of Current Interests in Psychology' which covered areas like personality, psychotherapy, religious beliefs and psychological qualities. All contributors were from European countries mostly from England.

The papers on the social significance of present-day trends included discussions on 'Trends in Government' and 'Trends in Science'.

3. Demography and Population Problem

A three-day session on "Demography and Population Problems" was held under the chairmanship of Prof. C.B. Fawcett of University of London. Thirteen papers were presented on the various aspects of Demography, viz. population of England and Wales, East Africa, and the Western Isles, Irish free States, the Ganges Valley, Ceylon, British North Borneo, Isle of Man. Migration and disease was another theme included in two papers.

4. Ethnography

There were four sessions on Ethnography, in which 65 papers were presented.

4.1. *Ethnography—General*

The four-day session on General Ethnography was under the chairmanship of Dr. A.C. Haddon of Cambridge University. In his introductory address, Dr. Haddon talked about the various forms of culture spreads. Dr. Haddon's address was followed by R.U. Sayee's talk on the same problem.

Nine papers were presented on the theme of 'Culture Spreads'. Some noted areas were : distribution of language in New Guinea; distribution of folktales; and oral literature. Included in this session were papers (12) on Indian Ethnography and short papers (8) on the Government of Native Races.

Contributors (12) on Indian Ethnology included B.S. Guha, Prof. R. Chanda, and K.P. Chattopadhyay (from Calcutta) who talked about race elements in India. It is significant to note that papers related to China, North-Eastern Malekula; Applied Anthropology in Papua; archaeological and ethnographic researches in Manchuria were placed in Indian Ethnology section.

4.2. *African Ethnography*

A four-day session was held on African Ethnography

under the chairmanship of Rev. E.W. Smith of London University. A total of 20 (19 English and 1 other) papers were presented on themes related to African Ethnography. This session included discussions on the essentials of the indigenous African culture (4 papers), Christianity and African customs (3 papers), African marriage, laws and customs and the effect upon them of contact with western civilizations (7 papers), witchcraft and colonial legislation (7 papers).

The prominent anthropologists working in Africa to contribute papers on the above themes included R.S. Rattraj, P.J. Schoeman, L.S.B. Leakey, Rev. F.W. Dodds, E.E. Evans-Pitchard, and Clifton C. Robert. Besides professional anthropologists, a number of other persons belonging to missionaries and the British army personnel were the contributors on African Ethnography.

4.3. *American Ethnography*

A four-day discussion session was devoted on American Ethnography including Central and South America, under the chairmanship of T.A. Joyce of London University. Sixteen papers (9 English and 7 others) were presented in this session. The papers were related to the following themes : Maya and Mexican writings; Eskimos; American Indian dance; African influence in Jamaica and in Dutch Guiana; Inca empire; archaeology of Peru; and methods of field research in South America. It is significant to note that of 16 contributors only 3 were from the American continent. The Universities represented were : Boston, Lima and New Orleans.

5. Technology

A four-day session on technology was held under the chairmanship of Henry Balfour of Oxford University. Twenty-one scholars (15 from English speaking area and 6 others) mostly from the European countries presented their findings in this session. The principal theories were concerned with ship-canoes building techniques; African crafts; pottery-making settlement types; sea animal teeth weapon; ornaments; primitive money; etc. The data were collected from the following places : New Hebridges, Peru, Beduin, Australia, Soloman Islands, Japan, Romania, Middle East, Chad, Eastern and Central Africa, and India including the Andaman Islands.

6. Sociology

A four-day session was held on Sociology under the chairmanship of Prof. C.G. Seligman of London University. A total of 34 papers (28 English and 6 others) were presented in this session which included 15 papers on rituals, 1 on law among the Arabs, 2 on clan and kinship system, 2 on culture contact, 3 on marriage systems of Egypt and India, 1 on the methods of analysis of sociological data and the rest were on other branches of sociology including Social Anthropology and Psychology.

As regards the representation of the country, mostly 25 were from the European Universities, 2 from India, 2 from Africa, 1 from the U.S.A. and the rest from Papua and New Guinea.

7. Religions

A four-day session was organised under the chairmanship of Rev. Prof. E.O. James of Leeds University. Twenty-five papers were presented by the scholars from all over the world. The major themes covered by these scholars were the magico-religious beliefs, the Sun-cult, confession and sins in primitive societies, totemism, cosmological beliefs, funeral, death and after life, divine king, etc.

8. Language and Writings

A four-day session on language and writings held under the chairmanship of Dr. Alan H. Gardiner of London University. The following were the broad groupings of 23 papers (19 English and 4 others) presented in this session:

1. The sociological study of words (4 papers)
2. The anatomical physiological, pathological and biological aspects of speech (3 papers)

3. Experimental Phonetics (4 papers)
4. Descriptive Linguistics (7 papers)
5. Other (2 papers)

III. CULTURAL PROGRAMMES FOR THE DELEGATES AND EXHIBITIONS DURING THE CONGRESS SESSIONS

On the concluding day, i.e. on August 4, many participants visited some of the places of anthropological interest in and around London. These included the universities of Oxford and Cambridge.

IV. SIDE LIGHTS OF THE CONGRESS : IMPACT ON THE WORLD ANTHROPOLCGY

From the scrutiny of the papers included in the proceedings of the London Congress we observe some important characters of the anthropological and ethnological sciences of that period :

(*i*) Anatomy and Anthropometry were integral parts of Physical Anthropology. Some important areas of Physical Anthropology represented in that period were Palaeontology, Osteology, Serology and Anthropometry. A region-based trend is apparent in these studies.

(*ii*) So far as the field of Ethnography is concerned, the popular areas of research were Culture Contact in Africa and Asia. The emphasis was on acculturative and synthetic aspects of religion and change, linguistic structure, folktales and megalithic problems.

(*iii*) Social Psychology was closely linked with Serology and Ethnology.

(*iv*) There were very limited studies done in the fields of Prehistoric Archaeology.

Publications

Reference to the volume on the proceedings of the sessions has already been made earlier. The British Working Committee of the First International Congress of Anthropological and Ethnological Sciences released a 340-page volume entitled "*Congress International Des Sciences Anthropologiques et Ethnologiques*" (Published by the Royal Anthropological Institute, London) 1934. This was the only published volume on the proceedings of the Congress.

2

The Copenhagen Congress: 1938

The Background

When the first ICAES took place in London in 1934, the Permanent Council consisted of representative delegates from 43 nationalities. There was an extended interest for the development of this Congress, and so three official invitations were presented : the first by K. Birket-Smith and T. Thomsen for the second Congress Session in Copenhagen in 1938, the second by W. Koppers for the meeting in Vienna, and the third by S. Sergi for the Session in Rome.

The Date

In 1937, the Permanent Council of the ICAES had its Preparatory Meeting on 8 May, in Paris where Copenhagen was selected for the second Congress Session between 1 and 6 August 1938. The office-bearers of the Congress consisted of the following :

PRESIDENT

Thomas Thomsen

VICE-PRESIDENTS

H. J. Braunholtz

Acknowledgements are to Dr. Anna Hohenwort-Gerlachstein for the assistance received for preparing this draft.

H. B. Collins
E. Fischer
E. Mauss
B. Schrieke

SECRETARIES-GENERAL

K. Birket-Smith
A. H. Brodrick
J. L. Myres

TREASURER

Kjeld Rordam

Members of National Delegation

According to the Report of the Congress 717 persons were registered : 555 full members, 162 associates, but only 527 were actually present in the sessions. Fourty-three governments were officially represented, and 186 universities, academies and scientific institutions sent their delegates.

THE CONGRESS IN ACTION

1. The Inauguration

The University of Copenhagen opened its doors on 1 August. In the large hall of the University, the inauguration ceremony took place which was honoured by the presence of the King of Denmark. After the national anthems of Denmark and Iceland were played, the President delivered his opening speech and declared the Congress officially opened. Then followed a number of official addresses in different languages greeting the Danish authorities and thanking them for their invitation. The delegates had come from Norway, Sweden, Finland, Germany, Turkey, France, Great Britain and Italy.

2. Organization of Sessions

The Congress had a rich and well organized programme. The great number of communications was divided into seven broad sections which were sub-divided according to the numbers and topics of papers.

Those sections were as follows :

1. Anatomic Anthropology and Bio-typology, Physiological Anthropology and Heredity.
2. Psychology
3. Demography
4. Ethnology
5. Ethnography
5.1. Ethnography and Folklore of Asia
5.2. Ethnography of Africa
5.3. Ethnography of America
5.4. Ethnography of Oceania
5.5. Arctic Ethnography
5.6. Ethnography and Folklore of Europe
6. Sociology and Religion
7. Linguistics and Writing

For the Plenary Sessions the following speakers had been selected :

(1) *Sylvanus G. Morley* (Washington, D.C.)
A Review of 25 years Research in the Maya Area of Middle America by the Carnegie Institution of Washington 1914-1938.
(2) *Niels Bohr* (Copenhagen)
Natural Philosophy and Human Cultures
(3) *J. Daugaard-Jensen* (Copenhagen)
The Old and the New Greenland.

A survey on the papers as printed in the *Compte-Rendu de la Deuxieme Session, Copenhagen* 1938, published by Einar Munksgaard, Copenhagen 1939, allows us a numerical classification reflecting the prevailing interests of that period and of the readers of papers. Physical Anthropology with its various sections had the best representation, then followed Ethnography of Europe, and Psychology. A comparatively small number of communications dealt with general ethnological problems. Reviewing the regional Ethnography, we notice that the Ethnography of Asia ranges first, while the other parts of the world like Africa, America and Oceania found only a few interpreters. In general, topics related to Sociology and Religion were better represented than Linguistics and Demography.

The section which should be significantly taken note of at this session was on Arctic Ethnography. Whether we read the paper by Diamond Jenness (Ottawa) on Prehistoric Culture Waves from Asia to America or the abstract by Henry B. Colline, Jr. (Washington D.C.). on the Origin and Relationship of the Old Bering Sea Culture, we can follow up from the stage of those days the background for the developing investigations of our days.

As Special Research Committees were concerned, we know only of two :

(1) The Committee for Standardization of Anthropological Technique.
(2) The Committee for International Research in Arctic Ethnology.

We noticed with satisfaction that Kaj Birket-Smith took the liberty of applying to the Congress for further support concerning his and the late Dr. Knud Rasmussen's plan to intensify an international investigation of the Polar tribes of America and the old world. This suggestion was welcome and a committee of leading authorities was put up in order to carry on the project on archaeological and ethnological lines.

Sidelight of the Congress

Every Congress Session is meant to be not only a place where reports are given on current Anthropology and future projects are presented but also an occasion to get in contact with all those colleagues whom we only know through correspondence and publications. In this respect the Copenhagen Congress offered to the participants all sorts of opportunities to meet and to talk because almost every day a reception or visit to a museum was arranged. Official receptions were given—

by the Director of the National Museum of Copenhagen

by the Director of the Glyptotheque Ny Carlsberg
by the Mayor of Copenhagen in the Town Hall

A banquet was arranged for the participants in Tivoli Gardens.

A lunch was offered to the associate members after they had visited the Rosenborg Castle where the crown jewels are exhibited. Another lunch was given by the Ladies Committee of the Royal Yacht Club at Langelinie after a guided visit to the Royal Porcelain Factory.

In all Museum Departments and Exhibitions special guided tours were arranged so that the visiting anthropologists and ethnologists could get a good insight into the local collections.

It was a surprise that four ethnographic films were one day offered to the Congress participants at that time, more or less a new attraction.

Cultural Programmes for the Delegates

In spite of the tight programme, the Organising Committee had managed to arrange three excursions during the Congress week :

(1) A city tour to see the historically important sites;
(2) A tour to the National Folklore Museum at Lyngby where prehistoric, mediaeval and recent Danish constructions are exhibited; and
(3) An excursion by autocars in the north of Seeland with a visit to the Kronborg—a fortress built in the sixteenth century—now Museum of Commerce and Navy.

Finally a visit to the Castle of Frederiksborg, now a National History Museum.

After the Congress, a tour lasting several days took the participants to a series of characteristic Danish monuments which are dated to belong to the Stone, Bronze, Iron, the Middle Ages and later up to our time.

Official Publication of the Proceedings

On the occasion of the second ICAES meeting, an official publication entitled *Congres International des Sciences Anthropologiques et Ethnologiques, Compte-rendu de la Deuxieme Session Copenhagen, 1938* was released which ultimately formed the only service material of this report.

Part Two

ANTHROPOLOGY IN A WORLD REBORN

3

The Brussels Congress : 1948

The Background

The report on the Brussels Congress goes back to Copenhagen the meeting place of the previous Congress. At the Closing Session of the Copenhagen Congress in 1938, invitations were extended by Germany, Portugal, Czechoslovakia, Mexico and Turkey to hold the next Congress in their respective country. But, hindered by the National Socialist Regime in Germany in the 'thirties, and the outbreak of the second World War in 1939, the meeting could not be arranged in that and other European countries. After the Armistice in 1945 and during the following years life slowly returned to normalcy.

It was during that period that ethnologists and anthropologists had started taking up coordinated research. In 1946, a call came from the Royal Anthropological Institute of Great Britain and Ireland, inviting the members of the Permanent Council of the International Congress of Anthropological and Ethnological Sciences to a conference in Oxford which were to serve to prepare for the next Congress. Obviously, it was the right moment to renew cooperation. Nearly 50 delegates accepted the invitation : the majority

---

Acknowledgements are due to Dr. Anna Hohenwort-Gerlachstein for preparing the draft on the Brussels Congress.

from Europe and a minor number from the Americas. The invitations, previously officially offered by Portugal, Czechoslovakia, Mexico and Turkey, were repeated and, unexpectedly, the Belgian delegation presented an additional invitation. Finally the majority of votes was won by Czechoslovakia, followed by Belgium. In 1947, however, the Ministry of Education at Prague was forced to inform the members of the Permanent Council that the Czechoslovakian Government could not possibly support a big congress within the following years. Belgium, however, saved the situation by declaring herself ready to arrange the Congress Meeting in 1948.

The Date

The session was fixed between 15 and 23 August 1948 and held under the high patronage of Queen Elizabeth. Presidents of Honour were :

Paul-Henri Spaak, Prime Minister and Minister of Foreign Affairs,
Cam. Huysmans, Minister of Education, and
Pierre Wigny, Minister for the Colonies.

The Belgian Committee of Honour counted 35 members, partly delegates from different Belgian provinces and cities, partly representatives of Academies and Universities.

The Secretariat of the Congress

PRESIDENT

Ed. De Jonghe

VICE-PRESIDENTS

K. Birket-Smith
P. Bosch-Gimpera
J.P.B. de Josselin de Jong
A.P.Elkin
H.J. Fleure
A. Leroi-Gourhan
G. Lindblom
R. H. Lowie

I. Schapera
O. Schlaginhaufen
W. Schmidt
S. Sergei
E. Tamagnini
F. Termer
J.A. Valsik
C. von Fuerer-Haimendorf

SECRETARY GENERAL

Frans M. Olbrechts

HONORARY SECRETARIES GENERAL

Sir John Myres
Kaj Birket-Smith

TREASURER

Fr. Twiesselmann

Members of the Belgian Organizing Committee

This Congress was organized by Dr. Frans M. Olbrechts and Dr. Ed. De Jonghe, and the Organizing Committee consisted of the following members :

J. Breuer
R.P.P. Charles
Henri Lavachery
G. Smets
E. Van Cempenhout

The Congress in Brussels and Tervuren deserves to be called an important event because it meant a new beginning of anthropological cooperation after an interval of 10 years with little or no communication among colleagues.

Six hundred individuals had registered for the meeting, but only 400 could attend the session. Thirty countries were represented—which meant an astounding number in 1948, actually only three years after the end of second World War.

Organization of the Sessions

As the programme comprised a large range, a comparatively wide spectrum of subjects was offered in the diverse sections. General topics dominated over ethnographic reports because, in those years, not many field studies were accomplished.

Physical Anthropology led in number, then followed Prehistory, Archaeology and Art, and finally Methodology, Sociology and Linguistics. Other worthy of mention general topics, treated in one or the other paper, were :

(1) Colonial History
(2) Cults
(3) Customary Rights
(4) Magic
(5) Museology
(6) Myths
(7) Oral Literature
(8) Philosophy
(9) Psychology
(10) Religion
(11) Rites
(12) Technology
(13) Witchcraft.

As for as regional or local investigations were concerned, no general line could be drawn because the various subjects in Africa, the Near East or in Madagascar, in India, Indonesia or Indo-China, in Australia or on the South Sea Islands, in South America or in Canada and among the Eskimos, were all of specialized natures.

Three decades have passed since the Brussels Congress. Since then the main interests within the anthropological sciences have undergone enormous change. Topics popular today had been slowly emerging at that time. Only a few of these should be mentioned here :

(1) Sona Rosa Burstein dealt with Gerontology and called "a field study of old age a serious desideratum in ethnographical research". (*cf.* Campte-rendu de la Troisieme Session, Bruxelles, 1948, pp. 34-36, 36-37)
(2) Melville J. Herskovits was following up Afro-American

culture contacts by analysing the Bahian Blacks in Brazil with a stress on comparative Ethno-Musicology. Afro-Bahian ritual music was then recorded during the field-work in 1941-42. (*cf. ibid*, pp.105-107)

(3) A Bojsen-Moller presented Synopsis and Film on the Expedition to the South Sea Islands on board the schooner 'Monsunen', 1933-35, through Panama Canal, the Pearl Islands, the Galapagos, the Marquesas, Somoa, Fiji, New Caledonia and the New Hebrides. Unique material was then collected for the Copenhagen Ethnographic Museum. (*cf. ibid*, p.22)

(4) Albert Eskerod from Stockholm read a paper on the Ethnographic Film as a means for urgent documentation. He complains saying that "only . . . the Northern Museum had made use of the film as a means of recording fast-vanishing forms of culture. There is doubtless a good economic reason for this, and I note with regret that the position is very little better in other countries." (*cf. ibid.*, p.79)

This report represents a limited survey on the Brussels Congress because no complete proceedings were published. All we have is :

(*a*) a collection of 36 Abstracts, edited by the Organizing Committee of the Third ICAES in Brussels, 1948.

(*b*) the *Compte-rendu de la Troisieme Session du CISAE, Bruxelles-Tervuren, 1960*, consisting of an alphabetic list of authors and a collection of 169 short papers read at the Congress—most of these papers were by contributors from Belgium, the Netherlands, France and England.

(*c*) *Juan Comas-Historia Bibliografia de los Congresos Internacionales de Ciencias Antropologicas : 1865-1954*. Chapter V : *Congres International des Sciences Anthropologiques et Ethnologiques* (CISAE) : 1933-54, pp.69-71. Universidad Nacional Autonoma de Mexico. Institute de Historia, Direccion General de Publicaciones, Mexico 1956.

The scarcity of material was due to the fact that the

Secretary-General, Prof. Frans M. Olbrechts fell seriously ill immediately after the Session and did not recover. Naturally under the circumstances, no one of the Organizing Committee inquired about the publication of the Proceedings. After Prof. Olbrechts' death in 1958 his wife handed over the material from the Congress to Mademoiselle H. van Geluwe, who started correspondence with the participants who had presented papers. Having collected all the material she could, Miss Geluwe abstracted it and compiled these in one volume of 277 pages under the title :

> *Congres Internacional des Sciences Anthropologiques et Ethnologiques*
> Compte-Rendu de la Troisieme Session Bruxelles 1948—Tervuren 1960

This volume she got published by L. Cohen, the Director of Museum, with a subsidy from UNESCO and the Friends of the Royal Museum of Central Africa. It was thus Mademoiselle van Geluwe's enterprise which allowed us at least some insight into the first post-war congress.

Part Three

THE AGE OF CONSOLIDATION

4

The Vienna Congress : 1952

The fourth ICAES was held from 1 to 7 September 1952 in the Institute of Ethnology, University of Vienna, Vienna (Austria).

Genesis

Soon after his return from the third Congress held at Brussels in 1948, W. Koppers, the leader of the Austrian delegation, reported about the acceptance of the Austrian invitation for the next Congress and invited his Austrian colleagues to take part in a preliminary conference concerning the planning of the congress. In addition to anthropologists and ethnologists, representatives of the allied disciplines were also invited to join in this venture. Thus, a programme had to be worked out before the Permanent Council held its next meeting in Paris in May 1951.

On 16 May 1951, the members of the Permanent Council of the ICAES assembled in the UNESCO House Paris under the Chairmanship of Prof. W. Schmidt. The Vienna delegation presented the preliminary programme for the next congress. The draft, in three parts, was discussed and unanimously accepted. The summary report, in three parts, is given below :

Preliminary decisions about Vienna Congress

PART I

(1) *Date of the Vienna Congress :* First week of September 1952 proposed

(2) *Staff of the Organizing Committee* :

President :
Prof. P.W. Schmidt
Vice-President :
Prof. R. Heine-Geldern
Secretaries-General :
Prof. W. Koppers
Prof. J. Weninger
Secretaries :
Dr. Anna Hohenwart-Gerlachstein
Dorothea Klimburg

(3) *Location* : Either only Vienna, or Vienna and Salzburg

(4) *Plan for Sections and Topics* :

(*a*) Anthropology, Palaeo-Anthropology, Methodology and theory, Anthropology of Races, Heredity constitution and blood-group investigations;
(*b*) General Ethnology, Methodology, Demography, Economy, Art and Music, Sociology, Psychology, Religion and Mythology;
(*c*) Regional Ethnology with film documentation;
(*d*) Cultural contacts between the old and the new worlds;
(*e*) Applied Ethnology and acculturation;
(*f*) Linguistics, Phonetics, writing with records of languages and songs;
(*g*) Prehistoric Archaeology and Ethnology;
(*h*) Folklore and folk culture;
(*i*) Anthropological and Ethnological teaching at colleges and universities.

(5) *Proposal for Arrangements*

(*a*) To give free admission to all delegates to anthropological, ethnographic, prehistoric and folklore museums and collections in and around Vienna.
(*b*) To prepare guided tours in and around Vienna for the delegates during the congress week.
(*c*) To prepare guided tours and excursions round Austria for the delegates after the congress.

PART II

Meeting of the Permanent Council of the ICAES.

Presentation of the Revised Edition of the Statutes, as prepared by a Special Committee in Paris in 1949.

PART III

Meeting of the Permanent Council of the IUAES.

Presentation of the Statutes and discussion.

Opening of the Vienna Congress Secretariat

Soon after the arrival of the Austrian delegates from Paris the Secretariat was installed at the Institute of Ethnology. The Austrian Federal Ministry of Education awarded a grant to the office to give it a good start.

The first step was to enter into contact with the local relevant University institutes, museums and scientific societies and solicit their collaboration from the beginning, in accordance with their interest.

The second step was the collection of world-wide address-material. About 12,000 invitation letters and/or first circulars were mailed between July and September 1951, to governments, universities, research institutes, museums, academies, scientific societies, besides a very large number of individuals. The second circular with a good survey programme for the congress followed in January, 1952, and the final third circular was distributed in June-July 1952, when all the details for the meeting had been fixed.

Finances

For the Congress Secretariat, the Congress Meeting, and the publication of the Proceedings, the following institutions awarded subsidies :

The Austrian Federal Ministry of Education
The Austrian Academy of Sciences
The Cultural Office of the Vienna Municipality
The UNESCO Headquarters in Paris
The Wenner-Gren Foundation for Anthropological Research, New York

It was of considerable importance for the Organizing Committee that a large sum was granted by UNESCO for travelling grants to be distributed to those delegates who had to play a unique role in the scientific programme. The amount could be divided up among scholars from Holland, England, Germany, Yugoslavia, Brazil, India and Japan.

The Vienna Congress in Action

From the very beginning, the Congress proved as one of the most important intellectual manifestations with international character at that time after the second World War.

At the inauguration ceremony, the Rector Magnificus of the University of Vienna, Prof. Dr. Alfred Verdross-Drossberg delivered the welcome speech, addressing the President of the Federal Republic of Austria, Dr. Theodor Korner, the Federal Ministers and Members of the Diplomatic Body and the official delegates of Governments, Universities, Academies and Scientific Societies, who had come from 51 states, beside the international audience of over 800 delegates.

The President of the Republic delivered the opening speech at the Congress, and expressed the wish that that week should turn out as an occasion for deepening mutual understanding among all those peoples and races that were present there, so that in the future it would contribute to the restoration and preservation of peace in the world.

In the speeches of the President of the Congress as well

as in that of the Mayor of Vienna, the high missions of Anthropology as the science for world peace were stressed in equal terms.

From 1 to 8 September the entire main building of the University was kept open to the delegates. There was the Senate Hall for conferences, the large Festival Hall and the Auditorium Maximum for Plenary Sessions, a great number of Lecture Halls, where the 20 different sections could be housed, another Hall for the Book Exhibition, two sitting-rooms and a restaurant.

In 1952, the wounds of the war were not yet healed. The country was still occupied by foreign troops. Many parts of the town had been bombed and had not yet been restored, and the outward appearance of the city was far from being the attractive old Vienna. Though in those post-war years, the Organizing Committee had to face great difficulties in preparing for the Congress, it may be stated with satisfaction that the Vienna Meeting meant, all the same, a new beginning in the History of the International Anthropological and Ethnological Congresses. It was not only the presentation of many papers with fruitful discussions but rather the valuable opportunity to get in touch with a large number of foreign scholars. One of the prevailing aims of the Vienna Congress consisted in the initiation of new trends in co-ordinated enterprise on an international scale. At the same time, Committees that had been inaugurated before found a new start on the occasion of the Meeting.

The Organization of the Scientific Sessions

According to the proceedings of the Congress published in 3 volumes (see Publications of the Congress) a total of 418 scientific papers were presented in several working sessions of this Congress. The following is the list of the number of papers with categorical classifications :

I. Plenary Sessions

1. Ethnology (7 papers)
2. Physical Anthropology—Basic topics (3 papers)

1. The Moscow Congress : Inaugural Function

2. The Vienna Congress in Action

3. Prof. P. C. Biswas at the Vienna Congress

4. Prof. P. W. Schmidt addressing the Vienna Congress

5. Prof. L. P. Vidyarthi and Prof. Newell

6. Prof. K. P. Chattopadhaya addressing the Vienna Congress

7. The Indian delegates at Vienna Congress

3. Urgent Anthropological Research (8 papers)

II. Physical Anthropology

1. Physical Anthropology

   (*a*) General topics (22 papers)
   (*b*) Specific topics (30 papers)

2. Palaeoanthropology (23 papers)
3. Biological Anthropology (39 papers)

III. General Ethnology

1. History, Methods (15 papers)
2. Religion (14 papers)
3. Art, Music and Dance (9 papers)
4. Cultivated Plants and Domestication (8 papers)
5. Education (6 papers)

IV. Regional Ethnology

1. Europe (36 papers)
2. North Africa and Near East (20 papers)
3. Africa (33 papers)
4. India (15 papers)
5. South east Asia (21 papers)
6. Far East (12 papers)
7. Australia (1 paper)
8. Oceania (5 papers)
9. Americas (39 papers)
10. European Prehistory and Palaeoethnology of Eurasia (19 papers)
11. Demography (5 papers)
12. Psychology (6 papers)
13. Linguistics (8 papers)

V. Film Projections

14 Films on various cultures

As it appears from the above, the majority of the papers were on Physical Anthropology which included both Palaeoanthropology and Biological Anthropology. This was followed by the papers on general and regional Ethnology. In the latter papers on North, South and Central America, Europe and Africa figure prominently.

The following institutions reflect international cooperation :

(1) The international Atlas for European Ethnography
Edited by : Prof. Sigurd E. Erizon (Stockholm)
Prof. Andre Varagnac (Paris)
Prof. Ernst Burgstaller (Linz-Austria)

(2) The Committee for the Standardization of Anthropological Technique
Prof. F. Frassetto (Bologna)
Prof. Mendes Correa (Lisboa)
Prof. Henri Vallois (Paris)

(3) The Organization of an international Conference for the investigation of European agricultural implements

(4) The International Committee on Ethnographic Film
Headquarters : Musee de l'Homme, Paris
Secretaire General—Professeur Jean-Paul Lebeuf

(5) The Declaration of the Question of Race—UNESCO
Presented by : Dr. Alfred Metraux (Paris).

(6) The Symposium concerning Urgent Tasks in Ethnology and Linguistics—An S.O.S. of Ethnology.
Chairman : Professor Robert Heine-Geldern (Vienna).

Proposals for the Re-organization of Congress Meetings

It was proposed that—

(1) aims and outlooks of every Congress be clearly planned and organized in advance;
(2) topics be selected and papers be accepted only if they fit into the concept;
(3) papers be sent in full length, and in time to the Congress Secretariat so that copies could be prepared before the Meeting and distributed to the participants who are familiar with similar problems and might act as adequate partners in discussions;

(4) an overloaded programme be avoided in order to save time for fruitful discussion;
(5) in every section chairmen be carefully selected, who are able to make full use of the material presented and summarize at the end; and
(6) communications presented be published in extenso and, if possible, with discussion remarks.

Sidelights of the Congress

When we look at the Proceedings of the Congress we notice the integral character of the anthropological and ethnological sciences as reflected in the contributions. Many papers did not deal with Anthropology or Ethnology as such but rather in connection with one or the other sub-discipline or allied discipline.

In Anthropology we come across the correlation of Anthropometry and Morphology, Anthropology and Medicine, Genetics and Paternity Test, or, Anthropology and Pedagogy, just to mention a few.

More coordination and mutual fecundation could be stated in Ethnology such as Culture, History and Ethnology; Ethnology and Philosophy; Ethnology and Religion; Archaeology and Ethnology; Ethnology and Psychology; Ethnology and Folklore; Ethnology in Education; Ethnology and Husbandry; and many others.

The majority of papers is connected with regional investigations concerning Culture-contact and change, acculturative and synthetic aspects of religion, tradition and change, sociological and linguistic structures, folklore, folk-art, megalithic problems, etc.

The spectrum of scientific information given during the Congress was not only illuminating in many respects but also encouraging for further fieldwork as quite a number of colleagues from the Third World extended their invitation to collaborate in the documentation of their communities.

Every Congress means a heavy task for all those who wish to profit from the occasion. Therefore it is the hosts' duty to fit into the programme some distractions and social events.

In view of the importance of the World Congress of

Anthropology in Vienna, the Austrian authorities favoured the assembled delegates by offering them two official invitations. One night there was a reception in the splendid suite of apartments in the Chancellery, given by the Federal Chancellor Dr. Leopold Figl and the Federal Minister of Education Dr. Ernst Kolb.

Another night, the Mayor of the City of Vienna Franz Jonas made a reception in the beautifully illuminated Town Hall. None of the delegates ever forgot the generosity of the Austrian authorities in those days in Vienna, when post-war restrictions and difficulties in everyday-life were not yet eliminated.

At the Closing Session on 8 September the President of the Congress thanked all participants for the intense work they had fulfilled during the Congress week. He extended his best wishes for their way home and expressed the hope that the sympathy they were displaying for Vienna and the Austrian nation may last also in the future.

The Official Publications

The Proceedings of the Congresses in London 1934, in Copenhagen 1938, and in Brussels 1948, contain only the papers read in the Plenary Sessions *in extenso*, while the other communications were just preserved as brief abstracts.

It was for the first time that the Vienna Committee managed to get all communications printed with photographs, drawings and tables. Abstracts were only added by those authors who wished to get their material published in some other place. The great amount of papers had to be divided into three volumes :

The titles of the publication read :

Actes du IV Congres Internacional des Sciences Anthropologiques et Ethnologiques
Vienne, 1-8 Septembre 1952
Tome I Anthropologica 1954
Tome II Ethnologica—Premiere Partie 1955
Tome III Ethnologica—Seconde Partie et Rapport General 1956
Verlag Adolf Holzhausens Nachfolger, Wien

The contents of the three volumes, filling 1082 pages, give a good survey of the diversity of subjects which prevailed at that time. It is out of question that the period after the second World War marked a turning point in our disciplines. When the colonial period came to an end, in one country after the other, new ways and means had to be found for investigation and documentation within autochthonous peoples and cultures in many parts of the globe. Therefore mutual understanding among many people of different nationalities at the Congress meant a new beginning for further cooperation.

5

The Philadelphia Congress : 1956

The Background

The Fifth ICAES was held in Philadelphia (USA) from 1 to 9 September 1956. The Congress was sponsored by the American Anthropological Association, the Ford Foundation, the Philadelphia Anthropological Society, the National Science Foundation, UNESCO, and the Wenner-Gren Foundation for Anthropological Research. A total of 295 papers were presented on various aspects of anthropological and ethnological sciences, viz : Physical Anthropology, Prehistoric Archaeology, Ethnology, Language and Folklore.

This Congress was sponsored by American Anthropological Association; Bryn Mawr; Ford Foundation; Longwood Foundation; National Academy of Sciences; National Research Council; National Science Foundation; Philadelphia Anthropological Society; United Nations Educational, Scientific and Cultural Organization; University of Pennsylvania; and Wenner-Gren Foundation for Anthropological Research.

The Secretariat of the Congress was composed of the following :

PRESIDENT

Froelich G. Rainey (USA)

VICE-PRESIDENTS

H. Baldus (Brazil)	T.F. McIlwraith (Canada)
Daryll Forde (UK)	A. Mendez (Panama)
B.S. Guha (India)	M. Oka (Japan)
K.G. Izikowitz (Sweden)	H. Petri (Germany)
R. Heine-Geldern (Austria)	A.H. Schultz (Switzerland)
H. Larsen (Denmark)	H.V. Vallois (France)

SECRETARIES

William N. Fenton
Alfred Kidder II

EXECUTIVE SECRETARY

Yvonne Oddon

DEPUTY SECRETARY

Martha T. Everett

TREASURER

National Academy of Science, Washington, D.C.

In addition to the above formal body, the local Organizing Committee consisted of the following persons :

Chairman :	F.G. Rainey
Finance :	C. Kluckhohn
Programme :	M.J. Herskovits
Local Arrangements :	Alfred Kidder II
Foreign Delegations :	H.B. Collins, Jr.
Sponsoring :	William Duncan Strong
Translation :	E.H. Ackerknecht
Members :	Loren C. Eiseley, A. Irwing Hollowell and Afred Metraux

The Organization of the Working Sessions

In the absence of any official listing of the Congress, other than one published volume in 1960, it is impossible to present a precise account of the number of sessions, names and number of institutions which participated in those sessions and other activities of the Congress. The only official publication pertaining to the Fifth Congress available to the present reviewer is *Men and Cultures* (1960) which contains 119 (40%) selected articles. These articles, according to Anthony F.C. Wallace, the editor of this collection, may be taken as the representative of the fields of Anthropology and countries which participated in the Congress. Fortunately Wallace's volume contains the complete list of the papers and the authors by whom presented at the Congress. The following summary report is based on these listings and full length papers included in the volume.

According to the volume entitled *Men and Cultures* a total of 295 papers were presented in the various working sessions. In terms of major broad grouping these papers may be classified as follows :

(1) Physical Anthropology—	28 papers
(2) Prehistoric Archaeology—	30 papers
(3) Ethnology and Cultural Anthropology—	183 papers
(4) Language and Folklores—	18 papers
(5) Papers presented on various aspects of Anthropology in languages other than English—	36 papers

In terms of the number of the papers the field of Ethnology and Cultural Anthropology figures prominently. The following is a brief account of the survey of the papers presented in various fields of anthropological and ethnological sciences.

1. Physical Anthropology

This major branch of Anthropology was represented by 28 papers touching the subject matter of Palaeoanthropology, Population and Race, Forensic Anthropology, human growth, Primatology, and Human Genetics. Some of the areas represented were Spain, France, Germany, USSR and Africa. Among the leading scholars in the field of physical anthropology who contributed their papers to the section on physical anthropology mention may be made of Mr. Fusteowd, L.P. Garcia (Spain); A.H. Schultz, (Switzerland); J.N. Spuhler (US); G.B. Lasker (US); I.S. Schwidetzky (Germany); Pierre

A. Vassal (France); J.S. Weiner (England); G.F. Debetz (USSR); R.F.A. Dean (Uganda); F. Nemeskeri and G. Acsadi of Hungary, Bozo Skerlj (Yugoslavia) and H. Suzuki (Japan).

2. Prehistory and Archaeology

This branch of Anthropology was represented by over 30 papers including those written in languages other than English.

Irwin Rouse presented a paper on the developments in American Archaeology; Gutoram Gjessing, on European Prehistory; Alex Krieger, on Archaeological Typology; C.L. Ramos, on Mesoamerica; J.H. Rowe, on Peruvian Archaeology; and D.B. Shimkin, on Western Siberian Archaeology. Besides, a number of papers were on prehistoric archaeological investigations carried out in other parts of the world, viz. Israel, Mexico, the Artic, Lebanon, Brazil, Spain, Bangladesh (the then East Pakistan), Indonesia and Africa.

In terms of country affiliations, scholars were from the USA, Canada, Denmark, and Mexico.

3. Ethnology and Cultural Anthropology

3.1 *General*

As was noted above, the largest number of the contributors (62%) were in the field of Ethnology. Some of the papers were on current status of anthropological and ethnological studies in various parts of the world. In this connection the papers on Current Trends in American Ethnology by Ralph Beals, Trends in British Social Anthropology by R. Firth, European Ethnology by R. Heine-Geldern, a joint work by Wen-Shan and Ho Lien-Kwei on Trends in Ethnological studies in China, I.I. Potekhin's Trends in Ethnology in the USSR may be noted.

3.2 *Theory and Methods*

Over 15 papers were on the methods and theories of Social-Cultural Anthropology. Linton Freeman's paper on Conflict in Anthropological Theory; C. Kluckhon's, on Typology in anthropological theory; David Landy's, on Methodological Problems in Ethnographic Field Techniques; George P. Murduck's, on Typology in Social Organization are of special significance since these were written by the noted anthropologists of the respective areas.

3.3 *Culture Change and Culture History*

Nearly 30 papers were on culture history and culture change. The related case studies were drawn from the Philippines, South India, Polynesia, North and South America, Jamaica, U S.S.R. and Middle East. While the majority of contributors were from the U.S.A., ethnologists and anthropologists from Norway, Vienna, India also presented their papers.

3.4 *Ethnography*

About 40 papers were on the ethnographic studies of societies of world wide. Some representatives were the Indians of North and South America, viz. The Pueblo, the Tapirope, the Tena, the Gautemalans, the Apache, and the Navaho. In Africa, the Ibo, and the Yoruba were the prominent ones. The Birhor, the Toda, and some peasant societies of South India and Nepal were described at length. Some of the important topics covered in these ethnographic studies were the inter-group relations, art and music, economy, kinship and religious beliefs and practices.

4. Applied Anthropology

Among the papers covering the field of Applied Anthropology the papers by Sol Tax on Acculturation, Laura Thompson on Applied Anthropology and Community Welfare, and G.E.J.B. Brausch on Applied Anthropology in the Belgian Territories in Africa (Central Africa) were of special interest.

5. Folklore

Ten papers were on various themes related to language

and folklore. Margaret Mead presented her paper on the framework for studies of folklores and survivals, Felix keesing on recreative behaviour, J.L. Fischer on structure in folktales and David McAllester on the role of music in western Apache culture were some of the important studies reported in this section of the Congress.

6. Linguistics

Among the papers on linguistics, mention may be made of the papers of Joseph B. Casagrarde's study on the comparative psycholinguistics, Paul L. Garvin and M. Mathiot's on language and culture, and Joseph H. Greenberg's on the classification of central and south Indian Languages.

A New feature

It was for the first time that the Soviet delegation participated in the World Anthropological Congress. With its emphasis on Marxism and Evolutionism the deliberations, particularly on African Ethnology, became quite lively and controversial. It, however, provided an opportunity for others to know as to what is happening in Soviet Anthropology and Ethnography. It also enabled the Soviet delegation to invite the next Congress in Moscow.

The Author's First Experience

It was also my first experience to attend and participate in this International Congress and get exposed to wider academic inter-actions. I still remember my long deliberations with Alfred Louis Kroeber, Clyde Kluckhohn and M. Herskovits who were considered until their deaths the unquestioned chiefs of American Anthropology. It was during such a get-together that I fruitfully impressed upon Clyde Kluckhohn to visit Chotanagpur which has one of the world's best anthropological laboratories. Such Congresses thus provide opportunities for exchange of ideas outside the halls which eventually open up new windows of research and scope of collaborations. Considering these, I made it a point to attend such World

Congresses, which, finally, culminated in my inviting the tenth ICAES in India.

Publications

As was noted above, the only publication based on the papers presented in the Philadelphia Congress came out in 1960, under the editorship of Anthony F.C. Wallace. This was organized by a Publication Committee consisting of Fredricka de Laquua of Bryn Mawr; William L. Thomas Jr. of University of California; and Anthony F.C. Wallace of University of Pennsylvania. The title of the volume was *Men and Culture, Selected Papers of the Fifth International Congress of Anthropological and Ethnological Sciences*, Philadelphia, September 1-9, 1956 (Publisher: University of Pennsylvania Press, Philadelphia, USA: 1960, pp. 810).

A Note on the Emblem Adopted in Fifth ICAES

It has been a custom at International Congress in the Science of man for Organizing Committee to adopt some symbol as the emblem of the Congress during that session. While the responsibility of selecting any object of fine art of the host country or especially designed drawing depicting the theme of the Congress goes to the Organizing Committee, efforts are always made that the emblem must convey something special to the Congress participants. Motivated by this the Organizing Committee of Philadelphia Congress adopted the aboriginal political symbolism of the League of the Iroquois: The Hiawatha Wampum Belt, a piece in the stone-age in North America.

6

The Paris Congress : 1960

The Background

The sixth ICAES was held in Paris (France) on 30 July to 6 August 1960. The venue of the Congress was Mus'ee del' Homme, Paris. The working sessions took place in the halls of the Palais de Chaillot, located in the premises of the National Museum, Paris.

The Secretariat of the Congress consisted of the following:

PRESIDENT

Prof. H. V. Vallois

GENERAL SECRETARIES

Prof. A. Leroi-Gourhan
P. Champion

MEMBERS

R. Gressian
H. Lehmann
Prof. C. Levi-Strauss
Mille Y. Oddon
G. H. Riviere

TREASURERS

R.d' Harcourt
Mme. M. L. Pasquino

EXECUTIVE SECRETARIES
Mme. M.de Fontanes
Mme. M. C. Chamla

The Congress in Action : Scientific Events of the Congress

Schedule of the Congress

The formal opening session of the Congress was held in the large amphitheatre of the Sorbonne, under the Honorary Chairman, the Minister of Education, at 3 P.M. on Sunday 31 July.

Working Sessions

The working sessions were held at the Mus'ee del' Homme and in two rooms of the Museum. All sessions were held from 1 to 6 August. On each day two sessions were organized : morning sessions (9-12 A.M.) and afternoon sessions (3-6 P.M.). Two evening sessions were held in addition at 9 P.M. on 2 and 4 August to accommodate more papers.

The reading of papers was on a half-hourly schedule which included both reading or presentation of papers and discussion.

A total of 111 sessions were held during the six-day conference in which 525 papers were presented. Of these 116 were in English and the remaining in French and other languages. The following are the brief notes on these sessions :

1. Physical Anthropology

This formed four sessions : *1.* Morphological Anthropology; *2.* Physiological Anthropology; *3.* Anthropology of Races and Population and Palaeo-Anthropology; and *4.* the Origin of Man. For the presentation of the paper each section held its meeting at various sessions under the secretaryship (Co-chairman) of one person. For each section there was a President (Chairman).

2. Morphological Anthropology

A total of 36 papers were presented in six sessions. Of

these, three contributors wrote in English. Because of translation difficulty, it is difficult to account for all titles of the papers. In general these papers related to methods, theory and interpretation of materials covering aspects of human skeletons, race-sex determination of crania, anthropometrografia, teeth patterns, etc.

The section on Physiological Anthropology included 29 papers which were presented in five sessions. Of these, three were in the English language. This aspect of Physical Anthropology covered human posture, sex-ratio, blood groups study, etc.

3. Anthropological Study and Population

There were 10 sessions in this section in which 60 papers, including 11 in English, were presented. Some principal topics covered were : vertebral structure of different races; racial diagnosis of individual racial elements in South Africa; the peoples of South-Western Asia; odontology and occulusion of the Eskimo; Australoid and tribal peoples of India; race structures of the Mongolian people and Saudi Arabia, etc.

4. Palaeoanthropology

In eight sessions, 43 papers were on Palaeoanthropology of which only four were in the English language. Topical subjects covered the problems of natural selection in man, neanderthals, pithecanthropine, dentitions, pleistocene man in Japan, and chronology of homo-sapiens.

5. Prehistory and Archaeology

This aspect of Anthropology was included in Section 2 of the Congress proceedings, but here, it is described under a separate category. There were 11 sessions devoted to Prehistory in which 57 persons contributed their papers. Of these 14 were in English.

Artic regions, Portugal, Balkan, India, Far East including Japan, Greece, Africa, South West US, Guatemala, the Middle

East and Israel, were the major places dealt with the archaeological studies.

6. Ethnology

There were 11 sections on Ethnology. Some sections of these were further sub-divided into various cultural areas. A total of 112 papers were read in 24 sessions related to Ethnology. The following are the papers presented in these sections and sub-sections.

6.1. *Ethnology : General*

In 5 sessions, 23 papers (7 English) were of general nature. Some topics presented were : continuities in communication; primitive man vs. homo-sapiens; egalitarian society; social control; heterogeneity and homogeneity in culture, etc.

6.2. *Ethnology of Asia*

There were 19 papers presented in five sections, of which 11 in English were on Culture and Society of Asia. The reported sub-cultural areas included peoples of Arabia, Kalinga in India, Pakistan and China. Kinship, marriage, family, totemism, caste system in India among others were the principal topics discussed.

6.3. *Ethnology of Europe*

27 papers (4 English) presented in 5 sessions were related to the European Society and Culture. Papers were on kinship system of slaves, special system of Balkans among others.

6.4. *Ethnology of Americas*

This section included 3 sessions in which 9 papers (including two in English) were on culture and society of North America and Central America including the Caribbean.

6.5. *Ethnology of Africa*

In 4 sessions 24 papers including three in English were presented on the African Ethnology. Papers were related to land and society of Ethiopia, Egypt, Congo, Southern Rhodesia, Nyassaland and Lybia.

6.6. *Ethnology of Oceania*

There were 2 sessions on Oceania in which 10 papers (4 English) were on various Islands societies of Oceania (New Guinea, Polynesia, Hawaii).

7. Technology, Economy and Material Culture of the World

In 9 sessions 52 papers (10 English) were presented on the aspects of technology, economy and material culture of various societies. History of agricultural techniques, marketing pattern, house building, among others were the main topics covered. It may also be noted that a few papers were on archaeology but included in the section of Ethnology.

8. Ethnobotany

This section was represented by 7 contributors who read their papers in this session. All the papers were in French language.

9. Ethnolinguistics

This included 4 sessions in which 19 papers (7 English) were presented on topics related to anthropological linguistics. Both descriptive or historical and semantic linguistics were covered by these papers.

10. Ethnomusicology, Art and Dance

23 papers (2 in English) were presented on music and dance of various cultures viz. Europe and Africa in 5 sessions.

11. Historical Ethnology and Folklore

This section was divided into three sub-sections : General, Europe and Africa. Altogether 8 sessions were held in which 46 papers were presented. Only two papers were written in English.

12. Juridical Ethnology

9 papers (1 in English) were related to political aspect of the society and were presented in 2 sessions.

13. Religion

40 papers (11 in English) were presented in 10 sessions on the religious aspect of the societies of different parts of the world. Conception of soul after life, folk rituals, initiation ceremony, *rite de passage*, ancestor worship, mythologies, popular religious sacrifices, etc. were the main topical grouping of the papers.

14. Ethno-Psychology and Medicine

12 papers (3 in English) were presented in three sessions and were related to Psychology and Medicine.

15. Culture Change and Applied Anthropology

20 papers (8 in English) were presented in three sessions in broad areas of cultural change and Applied Anthropology. The main societies or cultures dealt with were : Indian, Japanese, Chinese, Mexican, Austrian, African and American.

16. Museology

There were two sessions on Museology section in which nine papers (4 in English) were read. Among the main themes were : open air museums, monument preservation, archiving and presenting folk literature in museums.

Discussion Groups

The Organizing Congress Committee arranged discussion groups on some general subjects. The following were the subjects discussed in these groups :

1. Problems of ethno-genesis
2. Standardization in anthropological measurements
3. Common prbolems to Archaeology, Ethnology and History
4. Agricultural Ethnology
5. Music and Ritual
6. Juridical status of persons
7. Folk-tales
8. Games
9. Structural and semantic analysis of myths and oral literature
10. New religious sub-cretisms
11. Ritual food and drinks
12. Problems of Ethno-Botany.

Ethnographic Films

The Ethnological and Sociological International Film Committee (CIFES) organized film shows during the Congress sessions which were followed by lively discussions. Altogether 16 films were shown. These were related to land and people of Sudan, Oceania, Australia, Berlin, Spain, Europe, America and Asia including India and Nepal.

In their meeting the CIFES decided its future programme of research and documentation and the distribution of films in different parts of the world.

It is to be added that the film show was a continuous affair on each day of the Congress session from 1 to 6 August (morning and afternoon).

The Closing Sessions

On the closing day (6 August) the meeting of the Permanent Council of the ICAES was held. On the same day the meeting of the members of the IUAES was also held in which the representatives of the respective institutions participated.

A closing banquet for all members of the Congress was arranged on August 5 in the Pavilion Dauphine.

Post-Congress Excursions

The Congress Organizing Committee in association with Cook's Travel Agency arranged several excursions for the participants. This included sight-seeing in and around Paris river and other local excursions etc.

Other Events

1. *Photographs*

An official photograph was taken of the formal opening sessions of the Congress in the large amphitheatre of Sorbonne.

2. *Information Service*

To aid non-French speaking members of the Congress, a liaison and information service, with personnel speaking English, French, German, Italian, Russian, Portuguese and Spanish languages, was made available in the hall of the Museum. These personnel wore arm-bands, displaying the language spoken.

3. On the eve of sixth Congress a special booklet, entitled *General Information on Scientific Papers* containing entire schedules and list of scientific papers was brought out. It contained both the French and English versions of the statements.

Publications

The Organizing Committee of this Congress released a 94-page booklet entitled *Information Generales et Programme Scientifique* (Mus'ee de L' Homme, Paris) containing relevant information and titles of the papers presented in the various Sessions. The proceedings of the Congress were in French language.

PART FOUR

TOWARDS A RICHER MIX

7

The Moscow Congress : 1964

The Background

The seventh ICAES was held at Moscow (USSR) from 3 to 10 August, 1964. More than 800 papers, distributed over 27 sectional meetings, were presented by the anthropologists of more than 50 countries. The proceedings of the Congress were released in 11 volumes in 1968 in the Russian language. Each volume included more than 500 pages. Because of language barrier, it is difficult for this author to present a comprehensive account of the Moscow Congress. Some of his personal reminiscences are :

The Secretariat of the Congress

The secretariat of the Moscow Congress was consisted of the following personnel :

PRESIDENT
Prof. S.P. Tolstov
VICE-PRESIDENTS
Profs. H. Vollois
K. Jettmar
H. Collins
V. Correnti
D.A. Olderoggue

L. Pencot-Gracia
H. Suzuki

SECRETARIES GENERAL

Prof. G.F. Debetz
Dr. I.R. Grigoulevitch
Prof. A. Leroi-Gourhan

MEMBERS

Prof. L.P. Potapov
Dr. V.P. Yakimov

TREASURER

Dr. Mme. L.N. Terentyeva

SECRETARIES

Mme. M.G. Jouravleva
Mme. S.I. Neouronova
Mme. K.V. Yokimova (*Executive Secretary*)

Organization of the Working Sessions

As was noted above, a total of 828 papers were presented in the Moscow Congress. Viewing the themes and the contents of the papers, the Working Committee arranged as many as 27 sectional meetings to accommodate these papers. Each sectional meeting lasted one to three days, and two sessions—9 to 12 A.M. in the morning and 3 to 6 P.M. in the afternoon—were held everyday. On average, five papers were presented in each session. Each major sectional meeting was held under the presidentship of one prominent anthropologist or a scientist. He was assisted by a Vice-President and two Secretaries.

Following the guidelines of the Paris Congress, the Moscow Organizing Committee also arranged as many as 17 symposia. For each symposium, two persons were responsible : one, Chairman and, the other, a Secretary.

All sessions were held in the rooms of Moscow University which were opened for entry for the delegates during the Congress.

The Papers presented in the Working Sessions

Though all published eleven volumes are in Russian

language, the numerical classification of the papers allows us to prepare a brief account of the papers presented and discussed in the working sessions.

1. Physical Anthropology

Fifty-one papers were presented in the fields of Physical Anthropology. Of those, only 8 were in English language. From USSR alone there were 19 contributions. In this field, papers by Prof. P.C. Biswas of Delhi University and Prof. S.R.K. Chopra were also presented.

2. Human Somatology

Forty-two papers were on the theme related to Human Somatology. Fourteen contributors were from USSR. Only five papers were in English language.

3. Anatomy

Thirty-four papers were on Anatomy. Of these, 17 were from USSR alone. Only one paper was in English.

4. Ethnology

Forty-four papers were in the field of Ethnology. Of these, 13 were from USSR. Twelve were written in English language. This author was invited to present a paper on the history of anthropological development in India, a paper which was serialized in a revised form at regular intervals, and finally, provided the basis for his recent publicationns in two volumes. (*The Rise of Anthropology in India :* Concept, 1977).

5. Palaeontology

Thirty-five papers were presented on the various aspects of Palaeontology. Of these, 8 were in English whose authors were from the USA, South Africa, Japan, the Netherlands and France.

6. Theory and Methodology

Thirty-five papers (15 English and 11 others) were related to theory and methodology. Nine contributors were from USSR and 14 were from the USA.

7. Social Institutions

Thirty papers (6 English and 24 others) were on Social Institutions. Of these, 16 were from USSR alone.

8. Material Culture

Twenty-four papers (4 English and 20 others) were on material culture of the various societies of the world. Seven contributors were from USSR.

9. Prehistoric Archaeology

Thirty-seven papers were devoted to Prehistoric Archaeology out of which 13 contributors were from USSR. Seven were in English language; 1 from Canada and 4 from the USA.

10. Ethno-botany and Ethno-zoology

Sixteen papers were related to Ethno-botany and Ethno-zoology. Of these, 10 contributors were from USSR.

11. Ethno-linguistics

Seventeen papers (1 English and 16 others) were on Ethno-linguistics. Of these, 11 contributors were from USSR. Only two contributors were from the USA.

12. Folklore

Forty-three papers were on folklore and oral traditions. Fourteen contributors were from USSR. Four contributors wrote their papers in English.

13. Popular Music

Twenty-four papers were related to the aspects of popular music. Of these 10 contributors were from USSR. Only one paper was in English language and its author was from the USA.

14. Theatre and Dance

Eighteen papers (3 English and 15 others) were on theatre and dance. Nine contributors were from USSR and two were from the USA.

15. Popular Art

Twenty-eight papers (3 English and 25 others) were on the various aspects of folk-art. Of these, 14 contributors were from USSR.

16. Religion and Mythology

Twenty-one papers were on the aspects of Religion and Mythology. Nine contributors were from USSR. Five were in English language.

17. Applied Ethnography

In this field, there were 37 papers (10 English and 27 others). Ten contributors were from the USA and 7 were from USSR.

18. Human Geography

Twenty-one papers (2 English and 19 others) were on human geography. Of these, 10 were contributed by USSR.

19. Africa

Twenty-seven papers (10 English and 17 others) were on

African Ethnography. Of these, 8 were contributed by the scholars of USSR.

20. Oceania including Australia

There were 21 papers (14 English and 7 others) on the Ethnography of Oceania and Australia. Seven were contributed by the US anthropologists and four were by those from USSR.

21. South Asian and Oriental Societies

Thirty-seven papers (11 English and 26 others) were on aspects of South Asian and oriental societies. 14 contributors were from USSR. Eleven papers were in the English language and their contributors were from India, the USA, Japan, GDR and Nepal.

22. Occidental Asia

On this, there were 23 papers (2 English and 21 others). Of these, 13 were by USSR anthropologists. Only two contributors (one each from the USA and Denmark) wrote in English.

23. Artic and sub-Artic Societies

Thirty-one papers (13 English and 18 others) were written on the societies of Artic regions. Of these, 13 contributors were from USSR and 10 from the USA.

24. North America

Twenty-four papers (8 English and 16 others) were related to North American Ethnography. Of these, 7 contributors were from the USA and 7 from USSR.

25. South and Central America

Twenty-five papers (5 English and 20 others) were on

Ethnography of South and Central America. Five contributors were from USSR and five from the USA.

26. Europe

Forty papers (12 Russian and 28 others) were on the Ethnography of Europe. Twelve contributors were from USSR. All papers were in other than the English language.

27. Museology

Twenty-three contributors presented their papers on aspects of museum. Eight contributors were from USSR and 4 were from the USA. The papers written in English language were six.

Symposia

Of the 17 symposia, the major concentration was on nomadic culture; urban and industrial societies; agrarian societies; Ethnography and Anthropology of arid and arctic zone material culture; folklore and hominid origins.

During the Congress, a special session was organized to felicitate Leslie White, the noted neo-evolutionist of the USA, who incidentally received very late recognition in his own homeland owing to his continued researches in evolutionary theory. In addition, several special lectures on evolutionism and Marxism were organized in which selected specialists of the world participated.

The entire arrangements were regulated through the Institute of Ethnography of the USSR Academy of Sciences. Several receptions were arranged by the State, and the Soviet scholars looked after their colleagues quite hospitably, in spite of the language barrier.

On this occasion, the 35th anniversary of the Museum of Leningrad was celebrated for which several scholars, including this author, were invited to a special meeting held at Leningrad. The Organizing Committee organized several local tours to the places of historical and contemporary interests.

Publications

On the occasion of the seventh ICAES at Moscow, a booklet, containing activities of the Congress and abstracts of the papers, was circulated among the delegates. The detailed proceedings of the Congress in 11 volumes were released between the year 1968 and 1971. Each volume contained more than 500 pages.

8

The Tokyo Congress : 1968

The Background

The Eighth ICAES was held at Tokyo and Kyoto (Japan) from 3 to 10 September, 1968. This Congress, first one of its type, was organized by the Science Council of Japan under the auspices of the IUAES. A total of 1,136 persons covering 48 countries were the participants. Of these, 420 (the highest number) persons were from Japan, the host country. This was followed by the USA, which was represented by 274 delegates.

The Congress was inaugurated by the Crown Prince of Japan and, in addition to the delegates, it was attended by the distinguished audience drawn from the different walks of civic life of Japan and diplomats.

In his inaugural address, the Crown Prince extended a warm welcome to the delegates and dwelt upon the need of anthropological research for world peace.

In course of his presidential address, Prof. Masao Oka traced the evolution of Anthropology in Japan and highlighted its endeavour to integrate with developments in the World Anthropology.

Following the pattern advocated at the Sixth ICAES, held at Paris (1960) and the Seventh ICAES held at Moscow (1964), the scientific work of the Congress was divided into five major sections, (each section having several sub-sections) as follows:

1. Anthropology
2. Ethnology
3. Prehistory and Archaeology
4. Demography
5. Museology.

In addition, several sessions were devoted to symposia on some of the above sectional meetings. Special attention was paid to ethnographic films and to audio-visual aid in Anthropology and Ethnology. A further initiative of the Congress was the establishment of a number of working groups, such as for : (1) Urgent Anthropology; (2) Folk Culture—East and West; (3) Kinship systems of China, Korea and Japan; (4) South-East Asian studies; (5) Himalayan studies; (6) South Asian studies; (7) Traditional fishing culture; (8) Eurasian nomadism; (9) Anthropology of food and food habits; (10) International Biological Programme and human adaptability, etc.

Each of the above workshop was organized under a competent and interested person; for example, Sol Tax led the working group on Urgent Anthropology.

1. Anthropology

The section on Anthropology consisted of eight area studies : meeting of each was held under two or more Chairmen and co-Chairmen. A total of 106 papers were presented in the area-studies meeting. The following are the details of section on Anthropology.

1.1. *Theory and Methodology*

Ten papers were presented in the area of theory and methodology of Physical Anthropology, such as multivadiate analysis of human crania, standardization of morphognostic characteristics, somatology, micro-evolution, biogenesis, ergology, etc.

1.2. *Morphological Anthropology*

Sixteen papers were presented in the field of Morphological Anthropology. Changes in scapula, cranium, suture closure, squatting markings on the lower limb, upright postures, relationship between aging and the constitution, incidence of tablier, body composition and body growth, sex determination, Osseous characteristics of femur and tibia, radiologic study of brachymesophalangia, etc., were the topics discussed in this section. Contributors of this section were from the USA, Rome, the Philippines, Yogoslavia, Japan and USSR.

1.3. *Physiological Anthropology*

Sixteen papers were read in this field of Physical Anthropology. Some of the topics covered were : chemical structural analysis of triglyceride of the adipose tissue in man, adaptability of the response, high attitude adaptation, phylogenetic precursors of human sleep, fatigue, measurement of the enduring capacity of the erectors spinal muscles, locomotion restraint, etc. In this field the contributors were mostly from Japan.

1.4. *Palaeoanthropology and Anthropogenesis*

Eleven papers were contributed on palaeoanthropology. The topics covered were the Jomon period of Japan, homoerectus, neandarthals, homohabilis, Javaman, cro-magnon, trends in blood group determination, and pleistocene fossil remains.

1.5. *Anthropology of Races and Populations*

Twenty contributors presented their findings in the fields of race and population. Their research problems were related to in-group marriage and its consequences in Japan, racial composition of Egypt, Balkan, neolithic peoples of Europe, dermatoglyphics, Icelanders, Caucasus, Afganistan, skeletal remains of Bronze and Iron Ages in West Pakistan, modern population of India and Taiwan, races of northern Asia, tribals of Brazil and Venezuela, etc. In this field of Anthropology, the contributors were mostly from Japan, USSR and European countries.

1.6. *Human Genetics*

Nineteen papers were presented on the problems of human genetics. Some major topics included in this area were: distribution of enzyme characters in north Sahara population; blood groups in Mozambique, Libya, Ukraine (W. Europe), Ainn (Japan) ; findings of dermatoglyphics in pathological conditions, sexual variation in finger pattern size; sian colour among the Jews, hereditary factors in human growth; and the Beduins tribe of Sinai.

1.7. *Medical Anthropology*

Six papers were presented on the theme related to Medical Anthropology. Important topics included in section were: problems of mental health and individual personality; western medicine in the tribes of New Guinea, West Malaysia. Contributors were from Canada, the USA and Malaysia.

1.8. *Primate studies*

Eight papers were on primate studies, various aspects of primate studies included variations of blood protein in non-human primates; palm and sole patterns in baboons; locomotion and tool function of primates; age-sex groupings among pig-tailed monkeys, Japanese macaques; group-size distribution of the new world monkeys; etc. The contributors of primate studies were from Japan, Germany, the USSR and the USA.

In addition to the above eight sections of Physical Anthropology, six symposia were organized on themes of Pleistocene man in Asia (5 papers); dental aspects of human evolution (9); human posture and locomotion (9); selection and differential fertility (6); biochemical polymaphisms (7); and anthropological aspects of human growth (15). A total of 51 papers were presented in these symposia.

2. Ethnology

The sectional meetings of Ethnology included nine sub-sections and each sub-section was devoted to a major issue of Ethnology. A total of 224 papers were presented in nine sub-sectional meetings. Like the previous section on Anthropology, each sub-sectional meeting was held under the joint-chairmanships (two or more chairmen). The following is the detail of the topics covered in these sub-sections.

2.1. *Theory and Method*

Seventeen papers related to ethnological theory and methods were presented in the meeting. The major topical areas were : economic theory in anthropology; culturology; bio-social aspect of culture; structure of civilization; cultural relativism; complex society; data control analysis; video-type recording for ethnographic studies; and approaches to the study of marriage and divorce.

Contributors on theory and method were from the USA (6), the USSR, China, Netherland, Canada (3), France, Madagascar, Romania, Singapore.

2.2. *Cultural History*

Ten papers were presented on Cultural History. The important topical groupings of Cultural history were changes in the composition of the traditional field crops in Lavita, changes in the settlement patterns, ethno-genesis of the Ancient population of Asia minor; human sacrifice in ancient Peru; ethnic groups in China; and societies in ancient Korea.

2.3. *Social and Political Organization*

Thirty-one papers were presented on the themes related to social and political organization. The topical areas consisted of comparative method in Social Anthropology; sociological studies of small-scale societies, Urban Anthropology; kinship terminology; lineage systems; formal analysis of prescriptive marriage system; law of the Balts; Infrastructure of social behaviour; family system; dispute settlements; ritual kinship; and bilateral kinship system.

Contributors of this section were from Cyprus, Zambia, Canada (3), the USA (7), China (3), Japan (5), the USSR (4), Germany, Malaysia, France, India, Korea, and the Philippines.

2.4. *Social and Cultural Change*

Thirty-four papers were related to Social and Cultural Change. The principal topics covered under this were the dynamics of transformation; formal methods in the detection of change; changes in child rearing; kinship and urbanization; urbanization and social change; christianity, acculturation and assimilation. Geographical areas covered in these papers were : the USA, Japan, the Philippines, New Guinea, Thailand, India, the USSR and Brazil. The author, along with David Schnieder chaired the session on Urbanization and Social Change.

The contributors were from the USA (19), Canada (3), the USSR (3), India (1), Iran (1), Czechoslovakia (1), Germany (1), Japan (1), United Kingdom (1), the Philippines (2), Thailand (1).

2.5. *Economic Studies*

There were 11 papers on economic studies. The topical groupings of the papers were trade and market system; land reforms; agricultural practices; and fishery. These papers were based on the field-work done in Bering Straits area, Tokelau Islands, Papua area, Mexico, Taiwan, Thailand, India and Turkey. The contributors were from the USA (6), Canada (1), Australia (1), Germany (2) and Turkey (1).

2.6. *Religion and Folklore*

There were 22 papers presented in the section on religion and folklore. The topical areas covered were : ceremonial life of Mexican Indians; children's folklore; folk beliefs of Koreans; and myths in Australia. The contributors were from Rumania (2), Germany (2), Mexico (1), the USSR (4), the USA (2), Denmark (1), Venezuela (1), Korea (2), Turkey (1), the Philippines (1), Australia (1), Czechoslovakia (1), Norway (1), Iran (1) and Canada (1).

2.7. *Arts*

Sixteen papers were presented on 'Arts'. The topical groupings of this were : decorative art, house types, carvings, sculptures, prehistoric art, music and dance related to economic studies. In these papers the following societies and peoples were covered : the Gipsies, the Kazaks, New Irelands, Tibetans, Navaho Indians, African peoples, rural societies of France and Japan, and prehistoric societies.

The contributors were from Yogoslavia (1), the USSR (3), Australia (1), the USA (3), France (2), Germany (2), Japan (1) and Israel (1).

2.8. *Education and Psycho-Cultural Studies*

There were 14 papers related to education and psycho-cultural studies. Some subjects related to education and psycho-cultural studies were: ethno-psychology, tramp behaviour, personality and cultural theory, child rearing practices, language conflict, myth and world view, spirit possession, dreams and expectation and aspirations. The peoples and areas covered were city-dwellers of New York, rural societies of the Philippines, Mexico, Micronesia, Israel, South-West United States and Japan.

2.9. *Language*

Seventeen papers were presented on language studies of the world. Topical areas included in this were structural linguistics, figures of speech, descriptive linguistics, kinship terms, semantic analysis. The contributors on language studies were from Japan (7), Italy (1), the USA (3), the USSR (3), Hungary (1), Tahiti (1) and Indonesia (1).

2.10. *Material Culture*

Fifteen papers were on material culture of the peoples

and societies of different parts of the world. The major topics under material culture were : pottery-making, agricultural tools and fishing cultures. The societies and areas covered were Afganistan, Burma, Central Sahara, China and Czechoslovakia.

2.11. *Africa*

Twenty-five papers were presented on the Ethnography of Africa. These papers covered the following topics concerning peoples and areas : stratification in traditional Africa; female-office in primitive states; chieftainship in upper-Volta; Yorubas of Nigeria; societies of Ghana; African impact in Venezuela; Swazi rituals; foreign influence on the art of West Africa; Zulu mythology; and oral tradition in Africa.

2.12. *Ainu and Artic Region*

Six papers were presented on ethnography of Ainu and Artic regions; four papers were on cultural history and problems of the Ainu, and two papers were on the Eskimos.

2.13. *Japan*

Eleven papers were related to the ethnography of Japan. The topical areas covered were : the social systems of rural Japan; changing fishing communities; religion in post-war Japan; festivals in Japan; and folklores of Japan. The contributors were mostly from Japan.

3. Prehistory and Archaeology

Twenty-eight papers were presented in the sectional meeting of Prehistory and Archaeology. The major topical areas covered were as follows : dating the prehistoric sites and tools; typology of cultural sequence in Oceania; palaeolithic remnants in the New World, the Philippines and Japan; historic village communities in Denmark; air-photo Archaeology; Water Archaeology; American Prehistoric Archaeology; including Alaska, ceremonial architechnic in New Mexico; and archaeological research in Korea. The contributors were from the USA (10), Canada (2), the Philippines (1), Rumania (6), Denmark (1), Senegal (1), Japan (3), Dominican Republic (1), Czechoslovakia (1), and Korea (1).

Eight contributors presented their works in their native languages (i.e. other than English).

4. Demography

Twelve papers were related to the subject matter of Anthropology and demography. The topic-areas covered in these papers were ethnical castography, human environment, Applied Anthropology in South-East Asia, Japanese immigrants in Peru, urbanization and fertility, and population problems and family planning. Contributors were from the USA (4), the USSR (2), Rumania (1), Czechoslovakia (1), Egypt (2), Australia (1), Japan (1), the Philippines (1), and Yogoslovia (1).

5. Museology

The single paper presented in this section was on the National Museum of Ethnography of Sweden by B. Danielsson.

Symposia

Reference to the six symposia has already been made earlier (see section 1: Anthropology). Twelve symposia were organized on the themes of Ethnology, prehistory, ecology, planned cultural change, Linguistic Anthropology, analysis of complex societies, etc. The details of these symposia are as follows :

Symposium of Ecology in Anthropological and Ethnological Sciences

Twelve papers were contributed to this symposium. The subject areas covered in these papers were : concept of adaptation post-glacial changes in Northern Europe, from hunting to horticulture, shifting cultivation, and Ecology and business (Africa), subsistence Ecology and social systems, hunting Economy, genetical adaptation, and food habits of Australopithecines.

Symposium on Social Structure of Primates

In this symposium, five contributed their papers on social structure of primates. The topics discussed were : Biology of communication; rearing of Chimpanzee; fission in Japanese monkey groups; and social organization of wild Chimpanzee. Contributors were from Japan (4) and from the USA (1).

At the end of the symposium, a film on the social behaviour of baboons, made by Dr. I. Devore, was shown.

Symposium on Religion and Morality

Seven papers were presented in this symposium. The topical areas and peoples discussed in these papers were : Hindu Temples of India and Malaysia; Chinese and Japanese ancestor worship; morals and values of mediterranean islanders and the Australian tribals; and the concept of sin among the Kachin of North Burma. The contributors were from UK (3), the USA (1), Japan (1) and Australia (2).

Symposium on Formation Types and Acculturation of Eurasian Nomads

Nine papers were presented on Eurasian nomads. These papers were related to various aspects of nomadism, viz. research problems among nomads, semitic nomads in Asia, Japanese study on north Asian nomads, sedentarisation of nomads in the USSR, and origin of nomadism in Mongolia.

Symposium on Prehistoric Cultural Relationship in Northern Eurasia and Northern North America

Eleven papers were presented on theme of cultural relationship in Northern Eurasia and Northern North

America. These papers covered the following areas of research : the origin of New World ceramics as viewed from Eastern Canada; ceramics of North-Eastern Asia and North-Eastern America; Eskimo culture and its relationship to Northern Eurasia; palaeolithic culture of Kamchatka (USSR), sequence of palaeolithic cultures of Japan and their relationship with mainland Asia; and the problems of North Pacific sea hunters' culture. Contributors were from Canada (4), the USA (2), Japan (1), the USSR (3), and Denmark (1).

Symposium on Oral Tradition in African Societies

In this symposium the following topics were touched and discussed : folklorist approach to oral tradition; Japanese oral tradition and its application to African studies; reconstruction of past on the basis of oral tradition; genealogies for dating historic events.

The seven contributors were from the USA (3), Japan (1), Nigeria (1), Germany (1) and Togo (1).

Symposium on Planned Social Change at the Village Level

Three papers were presented in this symposium. The areas and peoples covered were New Guinea Highlanders, Fiji Islands under colonial administration, and rural societies of Taiwan. Two contributors were from Australia and one from UK.

Symposium on Culture Change and Psychological Adjustment

Twelve contributors (11 from the USA and 1 from Japan) presented their research findings in this symposium. The area and people discussed were Polynesia, Micronesia, Melanesia, American Indians and Eskimo, Arab societies and Middle East, the Burmese, the Indonesians, the Chinese, and the Japanese.

Symposium on Current Frontiers in Linguistic Anthropology

Six papers on Linguistic Anthropology were divided into

two main groups: Current trends in linguistic studies by Anthropology (2 papers) and honorific language (4 papers). The contributors of the former groups were from the USA while of the latter group were from Japan.

Symposium on Megalithic Problems

Five papers in this symposium dealt with historically inter-related cultures of a limited geographical area. Topical groupings under Megalithic were: Menhirs in South China, the use of stone by the Ifugao, Luzan, (the Philippines) and by Miyoko, Ryukya (Japan). The contributors were from Germany and Japan.

Symposium on Complex Societies

Four papers (3 from the USA and 1 from Nigeria) were presented on comparative analysis of complex societies. The topical areas covered were: family and kinship in complex societies, differential fertility in African (complex) societies, structure of complex societies and class conflict in complex societies.

Symposium on Ethnogenesis of the Japanese Societies

Four papers (3 from Japan and 1 from the USA) were presented on ethno-genesis of the Japanese societies. Approaches of physical, archaeological and Linguistic Anthropology were apparent in these papers.

Concluding remarks

In sectional meetings of Anthropology, Ethnology, Prehistory and Archaeology, Demography and Museology a total of 371 papers were presented. Eighteen symposia were held in which papers were presented. Moreover, the Permanent Council made certain significant amendments in the Constitution of the Congress which led to better integration of ICAES and IUAES.

Japanese Hospitality

The Organizing Committee organized lavish hospitality and served special dinners and drinks. The tea ceremony, the Ikebana exhibition and the trips to magnificent local shrines, temples and historical places both at Tokyo and Kyoto were generously arranged for the delegates. Special cultural events were also organized on some of the evenings which gave occasions to the delegates to acquaint themselves with the traditional Japanese cultural performing art forms, etc.

Publications

On the cccasion of the Tokyo conference, a volume, containing abstracts of all papers, was released. In subsequent years the Organizing Committee released proceedings of the Congress in three volumes, each containing more than 400 pages. Though these volumes were in English, papers submitted in other languages were also included.

9

The Chicago Congress : 1973

The Background

The Ninth ICAES was held at Chicago (USA) from 2 to 9 September 1973. The venue of the Congress was the Conrad Hilton Hotel, Chicago. The Chicago conference was one of its own type; the largest congress ever held in the field of social sciences anywhere in the world. Over 100 working sessions were organized in which about 1,630 papers were presented and discussed.

According to a statistical analysis, 82% papers were the works of industrialized countries including 15% Eastern Europe, 16% Western Europe, 47% North America and 18% were from developing areas. It is interesting to note that the works of developing areas (18%) alone were more than the total papers published after the last international Congress of Anthropology and Ethnological Sciences held in Philadelphia (USA) in 1956.

The Congress was mainly planned and organized by its President, Prof. Sol Tax. Dr. Margaret Mead acted as the Chairperson and exercised supervision for the successful implementation of the programmes. The Congress was inaugurated by an unknown member of American Indian tribe.

The Organization of the Working Sessions

In assembling this Congress programme, some specific techniques had to be employed. In response to the First Circular of 1971 the Congress staff analyzed suggested papers and sessions to see what actually interested potential participants. Some traditional topics, such as anthropometry, seemed not to draw much interest and fewer sessions were set aside for these topics. Paper proposals and session suggestions were analyzed into a broad, four-part framework :

1. Nature and development of man.
2. Looking at the world geographically.
3. Anthropological and ethnological sciences : Professional concerns.
4. Anthropological and ethnological sciences : Social concerns.

Within this framework of 104 sessions developed, some solicited but most from volunteer session organizers. These organizers were also expected to edit the papers they used to achieve a quality suitable for publication in the World Anthropology Project to follow the Congress.

The World Anthropology Project was one of the unique aspects of the Congress. First, the Congress aimed at becoming financially self-sufficient, and advances on royalties from book sales provided over a third of the Congress' operating expenses.

Pre-Congress Conferences

Thirty-six of the Congress sessions had associated pre-Congress conferences. These conferences helped the Congress in several ways. Many substantive issues could be discussed at length in the conferences, allowing time at the Congress to be spent on discussions in depth of major points, eventually leading to summary statements. Many conferences also had outside funding that brought participating scholars within a day's travel of Chicago.

Headquarters for the Congress were in a well known Hotel

in downtown Chicago. The entire hotel was reserved for Congress participants and all sessions except the inaugural Plenary Session were held there. Other accommodations were also available. Some 3000 persons participated in the Congress, with scholars from over 100 countries descending on the hotel. To try to minimize confusion a computerized registration system was instituted.

Figure 1 : IX° ICAES Quadrant Format

Nature and Development of Man

A look at the species both developmentally and in its present character and variety. From his origins among the primates the character of man is traced in all its dimensions—biological, emotional, intellectual, and "spiritual"—insofar as such distinctions are tenable.

A. Body and Behaviour
B. Mind and Culture
C. Expression in Man

Looking at the World Geographically

Anthropology of peoples and cultures through time (seven points of view selected for freshness and promise of international interdisciplinary interchange.

D. The Circumpolar Regions
E. The Pacific Rim
F. The Asian-African Hot & Cold Desert Steppe
G. The Indian Ocean Areas
H. China to the Antipodes
I. Europe
J. The Atlantic

Anthropology—Professional Concerns

The intellectual enterprise of the human sciences most broadly conceived, including: philosophical and methodological bases in relation to other fields of knowledge; changing research methods and techniques; problems of communication between specialities and with other scholars and the public; worldwide problems of information control, of relating to political powers and the general public. It is here that all methodological arguments within the discipline of "how scientists uncover knowledge" are focused.

K. Theoretical Perspectives
L. Data Storage and Retrieval
M. History and Future of Anthropological Sciences

Anthropology—Social Concerns

The uses of knowledge of the human sciences at all levels—from deeper understanding to assistance in solving specific social problems. On the one side there is consideration of three problems affecting the whole species with varying interpretations of their nature and possible outcomes. On the other side there are the specific problems of modern urban societies, as exemplified in selected cases in "aspects of social life."

N. Species Problems
O. Fates of Indigenous and Minority Peoples
P. Aspects of Social Life
Q. The Future

The Congress opened and closed with Plenary Sessions emphasizing the theme of the Congress, "One Species—Many Cultures". The Opening Plenary Session on September 1, 1973 began with a presentation by the Chicago Childrens' Choir. Dr. Tax welcomed the assembly, introduced the Permanent Council and announced that India would be the site of the Tenth Congress in 1978. After Dr. Vidyarthi's speech the American Folk Concert singers were introduced, Native American activist Vine Deloria welcomed the assembly, and he was followed by Lawrence Krader and Margaret Mead.

Scientific sessions took place in four large rooms in the Hotel where people were staying, but when scholars arrived they did not usually find someone reading aloud over a loud-speaker. Ideally, they found informed discussion, with simultaneous translation into four languages, of a paper which had been distributed beforehand. For the Ninth Congress 1200 packets of papers were mailed in advance to participants. This was not enough advance distribution to completely accomplish its goals, but the gap was filled somewhat by the discussion of papers at pre-Congress conferences. The largest simultaneous translation effort ever undertaken was more successful.

The profusion of papers, some 2,200 in all, balanced each other and filled the four-part framework (Fig. 1). There were too many major advances in the various fields to discuss them here, and the World Anthropology Project stands as an index of the success of the academic sessions.

The Working Sessions of the Congress

According to the Abstract volume entitled *International Congress of Anthropological and Ethnological Sciences* (*1973*), as many as 104 sectional meetings (sessions) were organized, covering all imaginable subjects of human behaviour. It is to be noted that the Chicago Congress was planned from the very beginning not only to include as many of the scholars from every part of the world as possible, but also with a view towards their eventual publication in volumes. Scholars were asked both to propose topics of their own and to suggest topics for sessions of the congress which they might edit into volumes. It is not then surprising that 104 topical groupings were chosen as individual sectional meetings.

In recording and describing these papers we shall follow the previously noted major categories, i.e. Nature and Development of Man or Physical Anthropology; Looking at the World Geographically; Pre-History and Archaeology; Professional concerns of Ethnology; and the social concerns.

A considerable effort has been made to bring together papers presented under different sections in the broad categories noted above although it is possible that some subjects may be regarded by their authors as belonging to more appropriately to another section.

The main source of preparing the outline of the papers presented at the Chicago Congress has been, as noted above, the Abstract volume released on the occasion. The followings are the details of the various working sessions :

1. Physical Anthropology

A total of 14 sessions were held on Physical Anthropology. As many as 255 papers were presented and discussed in those sessions. Of these 219 were in English and 36 in other languages.

The following is a brief account of the sessions held and papers presented.

1.1. *Methods and Perspectives in Human Biology*

19 papers (15 English and 4 others) were presented in this session. Anthropometric measurement, somototype patterns in Melanesia, interpopulation variability, etc. were some topics among others on which papers were presented.

1.2. *Physiological and Morphological Variation and Adaptation*

1.3. Included in this session were 9 papers (7 English and 2 others) related to bio-social adaptation. Physical adaptation of prehistoric population and the problem of ethnogenesis were some topics discussed in these papers.

1.4. *Genetic factors in Human Differentiation*

51 papers (43 English and 8 others) were on human genetics, discussion was planned around two major ideas first, polymorphic variation in terms of micro-evolution, and second, the critical and speculative position concerning the relevance to human evolution of the issues of mutation, non-Darwinian group selection and cybernetic models.

1.5. *The Physical Anthropology of Pre-Historic Populations*

28 papers (24 English and 4 others) were presented on aspects of the Physical Anthropology of early and later populations around the world, with emphasis on osteological, dentition and palaeoserological evidence. Places to which papers referred were Europe, Harappa, Egypt, Baltic, Americas, Portugal, Australia, Czechoslovakia and Africa.

1.6. *Palaeoanthropology: Behaviour*

23 papers (21 English and 2 others) were presented in the session on Palaeoanthropology. The themes of the papers were centred around the meaning of formal similarity and diversity in pre-historic artefacts, pre-historic subsistence and settlement strategies and analytical method. Data in these papers were drawn from prehistoric sites of Israel, the Mediterranean Basin, the Middle East, Southern Africa, North Africa, East Anglia, Spain, Balkans, Asia and Lebanon.

1.7. *Palaeoanthropology : Morphology and Palaeoecology*

In this session 20 papers (19 English and 1 other) were read and discussed. The papers were on pleistocene hominoids. Findings on hominoids were related to new perspective on speciation, sexual dimorphism, diet, and life ways.

1.8. *Dermatoglyphics*

8 papers (7 English and 1 other) were on the various

aspects of a worldwide study of finger prints. Data on these papers were drawn from the populations of India and Hungary, among others.

1.9. *Primates : Chromosomes and Evolution*

6 papers (5 English and 1 other) were on primate chromosomes with a view to interpret genetic information in human chromosomes.

1.10. *Primates : Functional Morphology and Evolution*

A second session was devoted on Morphology and Evolution of catarrhine primates in which 25 papers (21 English and 4 others) were presented. Feeding behaviour, bipedalism, knuckle walking, human language, etc., were the themes to which these papers referred.

1.11. *Primates : Socio-Ecology and Psychology*

A third session was also arranged on the primates in which 20 papers (19 English and 1 other) were presented. These papers referred to Ecology, diet, social paternity in monkeys and apes. Besides capacities for learning, symbolizing and language skills in apes and the evolution of language were discussed.

1.12. *Dental Anthropology*

27 papers (26 English and 1 other) were on Dental Anthropology. Importance of genetic and environmental backgrounds in the evolution and understanding of dentitional and oro-facoab urpobems of growth and development. These papers were related to studies done in Alaska, Canada, Easter Island, Australia, China, Japan and Europe.

1.13. *Physical Anthropology in Europe*

13 papers (8 English and 5 others) were directly related to the physical anthropological studies in Europe. This

included a series of discussion on palaeoanthropological, serological and constitutional data on European and related papers.

1.14. *Population Differentiation and Palaeopathology along the American Cordilleras*

6 papers (5 English and 1 other) were on population differentiation in the new world in terms of genetics, serology, osteology, etc. Some papers dealt with palaeopathology and palaeoserological studies. The related case-studies were reconstructed on the materials from Peru, Bolivia and the USA.

2. Pre-historic archaeology

There were seven sessions in 49 papers in which (38 English and 11 others) related to pre-historic Archaeology were presented. The following is the brief account on each of these sessions.

2.1. *Lithic Technology*

Eight papers involved historical, experimental, analytical and theoretical discussions on lithic cultures of worldwide. Some data of the papers were drawn from pre-historic sites of Spain, Northern Chile, China and Florida (USA).

2.2. *Origins of Agriculture*

Four papers presented in the session on pre-history were related to the origin and development of agriculture. The reported sites were Eastern and South-East Asia, African Savanna, North Mexico and the Andes.

2.3. *African Plant Domestication*

Two papers were about the origins of plant domestication in Africa.

2.4. *Pre-historic Cultural Adaptation in Western North America*

Nine papers were related to western North American

prehistoric Archaeology. The contributors looked for new evidence for early man in North America.

2.5. *Early Man in Siberia and New World*

Twelve articles were presented on Siberian migration prior to 10,000 B.P. (Before present) studies were based on evidences collected from the New World.

2.6. *Early Palaeolithic of East Asia*

Eight papers were on early palaeolithic cultures of Indonesia, Burma, India, Pakistan, Korea and Mongolia.

2.7. *Later Pre-History of the Circumpolar Regions*

Six papers on later palaeolithic migration and of the people inhabiting circumpolar region. Data, on which these papers were based, were drawn from European points of USSR, North Pacific Coast and Alaska.

3. Ethnology

Two hundred and fifty-two papers (225 English and 27 others) presented in 18 sessions were, for the present analysis, classified in the category of Ethnology. These were related to theory and method in Cultural Anthropology, land and people of almost all continents. A short description of the paper included in these sessions may be described as follow :

3.1. *Ethnology : General Methods and Theories*

Twenty-two papers (21 English and 1 other) were presented on ethnological theories and methods. Some of these papers were written on themes like national character, Ecology and Man, American cultural values, concept of Culture, epistemological remarks on Social Anthropology, Pan-culture, social organization, depth research, explanation in Anthropology, inter-disciplinary approaches in Anthropology, etc.

3.2. *Problems and Possibilities of a Marxist Ethnology*

Fifteen papers were devoted to Marxist insights into ethnological materials. These studies were: relevance of economic theory; social stratification; Piaget and Marx, Marxist theory of History ; social evolution; feudalism; and Mao Tse-Tung's dialectical method.

3.3. *Europe : Anthropology and Ethnology*

Thirty papers (23 English and 7 others) contained ethnological studies related to Europe. The underlying theme of these papers was to explore aspects of cultural history, archaeology and contemporary situation of various European cultures. Data of these studies were drawn from Hungary, Romania, Sweden, Bolivia, Turkey, France, Ukranian and Sarakatsani cultures.

3.4. *Northern Atlantic Europeans*

Fourteen papers (12 English and 2 others) were on the study of Ecology, Economy, social structure and social change in Northern Atlantic maritime European of Mid Coast Maine, New Foundland, Adriatic Coast and Portugal.

3.5. *Europe : The Atlas and its Significances*

One session was devoted on the progress of the European Atlas to date. Four papers (3 English and 1 other) were presented in this session.

3.6. *Bridging Old and New World : Maritime Adaptation*

Fourteen papers were contributed to the studies related to pre-historic and ecological adaptation in the circumpolar regions of the old and New World with special reference to the culture of coastal populations. Data were drawn from studies done in Alaska, Northern Sweden, Norway, Scandinavia, the North-Western Atlantic Coast, North Pacific Coast, and the Baltic.

3.7. *The American Cordillers : Population Differentiation and Palaeopathology*

Eight papers (5 English and 3 others) were on palaeopathology and human biology of peoples along with the Cordillers and neighbouring areas of North and South America. Some of the populations represented in these papers were tribal societies of Peru and peasants of Mexico and Bolivia.

3.8 *Cultural History and Socio-political Evolution in the Andes and Amazonia*

Fourteen papers (11 English and 3 others) were presented on the cultural history of the Andes and Amazonia which included economic and political interaction among the peoples, trade networks, development of state. of agriculture and animal husbandry, palaeoecology, palaeobotany, new techniques in lithic and ceramics analysis and relationships between indigenous and Spanish populations in the colonial period. The various case-studies were reported from Peru, Venezuela, Chile, the Amazon, Argentina, Equador, and South Western United States.

3.9 *Cultural Continuity in Meso America : Pre-historic and Ethno-historic studies*

Seven papers (5 English and 2 others) were based on the pre-historic and ethno-historic studies done in various parts of Central America. These papers explored the origin and development of state in Meso-America, pre-columbian writing systems, Aztec and Mayan religious concepts, the Carribean cultural development, Aztec and later colonial ethno-history, and Meso-American interaction spheres and their art styles. The field data were drawn from Central Costa Rica, Mayan and Olmec culture.

3.10 *Maritime Anthropology : The Pacific*

Eight papers were presented on various aspects of Man's relation to the sea in Oceania and the pacific from pre-historic times to the present. Data of these papers were collected from Southern New Zealand, the Soloman Islands and the Pacific Coast dwellers.

3.11. *Polynesia and Micronesia*

Aspects of polynesian pre-historic, traditional cultures, and modern social, economic and political situations were discussed in a separate session in which 5 papers (3 English and 2 others) were presented. Data, on which these studies were based, were drawn from Southern New Zealand, South Pacific, Samoa, Northern Aarians (Indonesia) and Tonga.

3.12. *Melanesia*

Six papers were presented on the peoples and cultures of Melanesia. Subjects covered in these studies were Physical Anthropology, cultural history and current problems of ethnographic field works, field works of the Soloman Island, the Sepik area, Papua and New Guinea, Soromajal (West New Guinea) and the Moklai Coast.

3.13. *Australia and Tasmania*

Three papers were on the culture area of Australia and Tasmania. The papers presented were related to early Australian lithic industries, Tasmanian origins, Australian kinship system and aboriginal contact with the outsiders.

3.14. *Anthropology of South-East Asia*

The session on anthropological studies in South-East Asia included 12 papers. These papers covered a wide range of subjects, viz. administration of the native tribes of Western Malaysia, ceremonial relationships in the Philippines communities, the Japanese and Chinese populations of Thailand, social mobility in Combodia, kinship system of the Philippines, Malaya migration to Kuala Lumpur city, folklore and matrilineal societies of South-East Asia and Cultural Anthropology in the Philippines.

3.15. *The Himalayan Interface*

The subject matter of 27 papers (26 English and 1 other) was related to the Himalayan region. The main aim of this session was to examine the important cultural traditions which survive around the Himalayas in their ecological and historical perspective. Studies done in rural Nepal including the Newars of Kathmandu and Tibet found special prominence. As a matter of fact more than a dozen papers were on cultural history of Nepal.

3.16. *Anthropology of the Far East*

A general anthropological overview of the Far East was the central theme of the session on Anthropology of the Far East in which 24 papers (23 English and 1 other) were presented. These papers were related to the aspects of Chinese kinship system, languages of Taiwan, palaeolithic of the Far East, cave burial in Japan, tribal music, Shaminism in Taiwan, Chinese mythical legends, festivals of rituals of Japan, kitchen medden in central Korea cults among the Puyuman and the Miyako Islanders, changes in Mongolian philosophy of life, kinship terminologies of the Okinawans, and Japanese art and oral liteıature. In addition, two papers were on Mao's concept of 'investigation' and his philosophy.

3.17. *Circumpolar Peoples*

Twenty-four papers were on cultures of the inhabitants of circumpolar region. These papers were based on the ethnographic facts related to south Siberia. North West of South Soknalin, Soviet Pacific and northern regions of the Baltic. Subjects covered in these studies were ethnography of Eskimos, Ainu, Ojibwu's cannibalism, bilingualism and prehistoric culture.

3.18. *Asian, African Hot and Cold Desert and Steppe*

Twenty-four papers (20 English and 4 others) examined prehistoric cultures, historical and contemporary cultures of the peoples of Asian-African hot and cold desert Steppe regions. Data for these papers were drawn from nomads of the Middle East, cattle breeders of Soviet Eastern Republics, South-Eastern Asia, Afghanistan, Northern India, Asiatic and African nomads.

4. Folklore and Art

Five sessions were organized on the various aspects of studies of folklore and studies of art of the peoples of world. A total of 105 papers (89 English and 16 others) were presented in these sessions. A brief note on each of these session is as follows :

4.1. *Structure of Oral Literature*

Fifteen papers (14 English and 1 other) were presented in the session on the structure of oral literature. Some of the papers were related to theoretical assumptions and structural analysis of folklore. While in some papers, case studies were collected from France, Denmark, USSR, Hebrew, Turkey, and the USA, the others were purely theoretical in nature.

4.2. *Folklore in the Modern World*

Twenty-eight papers (19 English and 9 others) were related to the folklore in the changing world. Case studies were collected from parts of Europe, Kentuky (the USA), North India, Turkey, Egypt, Africa, and Peru and other places of Latin America and South-East Asia.

4.3. *Folklore*

Four articles were written on the aesthetic aspects of folklore and its role in society as a key to cognitive system.

4.4. *The visual arts*

Fifteen papers (5 English and 10 others) were presented and discussed in the session on the visual arts. These studies were related to graphic and plastic art forms, architecture, city planning, customs, etc., covering the entire world. The related case-studies were drawn from northern Nigeria, Iran, Yogoslavia, India, Poland, Czechoslovakia, Mexico, the USSR, South Pacific and the USA.

4.5. *Attentive response in man : The performing arts*

Thirty-six papers (35 English and 1 other) were presented on the themes related to music, dances, theatre, pageantry and stoıy-telling of various cultures of the world, viz., Hungary, Africa, Southeast Asia, Libya, Venezuela, the USSR, Taiwan, Turkey, Yogoslavia, Jamaica, Peru, Korea and China.

4.6. *Museology*

One session was organized on ethnological museology in which four papers were presented. Topics discussed in these papers were problems of cartography in ethnography, research role of museums, exhibitory African art and ethnographical peculiarities of Solvenia.

5. Research in Methodology including Visual Aids

Two sessions were organized on the aspects of research methodology including visual aids in Anthropology. A total of 20 papers were read and discussed in these sessions.

6. Bibliography and Documentation

Two papers (1 English and 1 other) were on the use of library research in Anthropology.

7. Visual Anthropology

One session in which 18 papers (17 English and 1 other) were presented was devoted to recent problems in the application of film-making to Anthropology and to the use of film in ethnographic documentation, body-behaviour studies, reconstructing cultures through film, and the use of film materials in the class room. Visual aids included photography, film, videotape and T.V.

8. Political anthropology

8.1. *Political Anthropology and the State*

Seventeen papers (16 English and 1 other) were related to the political processes involved in authority relations between state centres and their peripheral sectors. Besides some papers were on the development of Political Anthropology as a comparative ethnological approach to political systems. The related case-studies were drawn from primitive states, viz. Dohomey, Hawaii, Tonga, Tahiti, Buganda, and Incas, Uroan Swellers of South Africa, Trinidad, Indonesia, the USA and Mexico.

8.2. *Society and Politics at the National Frontier*

Fourteen papers were on the theme of interrelation between society and politics. While some papers were theoretical and conceptual in nature, others were based on the field work done in South India, Israel, Afghanistan, Siberia, and among the American Indians of the USA.

9. Cultural Practices

Under this section are included some of general topics of anthropological interest, viz., the cannabis, food habits, communal living, etc. Individual sessions were arranged for each of these broad topics. The following is an account of the papers included in these sessions :

9.1. *Cross Cultural Perspectives on Cannabia*

Seven papers (6 English and 1 other) examined the persent state of knowledge on the patterns of use of cannabis in historical and cultural contacts. Patterns in cannabis use in Rwanda were reported in these papers.

9.2. *Anthropology of Food and Food Habits*

Nineteen papers (18 English and 1 other) were on the subjects related to food and food habits from several perspectives, folklore, culture, history, social anthropology, ethnology, and nutritional science. The related case-studies, reported in these papers were collected from Greek, the Balkans, the Yamen, African, South and North American Indians, the Pacific Islands and the Mexican American societies.

10. Medical Anthropology

The subject matters of 51 papers fell in the jurisdiction of Medical Anthropology which covered the topics such as culture bound healing practices, anthropologists' roles in health services, interactions between the Western and non-Western medicinal practices, and problem of mental health. These papers were divided into three sessions. A brief note on these sessions is as follows :

10.1. *Medical Anthropology*

Twenty-one papers (20 English and 1 other) were related to the aspects of Medical Anthropology. Some topics discussed were : sexual basis of illness; science, witchcraft and medicine; folk medicine; alcoholism; religion and science; social biology; ancestor cult and sufferings; African traditional medicine and medical care in societies of cross-cultures. The related case-studies were drawn from the field-work completed in Gautemala, Brazil, Nepal, Argentina, Canada, Africa, Japan and the USA.

10.2. *Health care Policy Studies*

Five papers were presented on the health care policy of the USA, Canada, Argentina and socialist countries, such as China, Chile, Cuba and Tanzania.

10.3. *Anthropology and mental health*

Twenty-five papers (24 English and 1 other) were on cross

cultural perspectives on intersections of anthropology and problems of mental health. The related case studies were drawn from India, Africa, Central America, the USA and the Philippines.

11. Religion

Two sessions were held on religion in which 81 papers related to religious beliefs and practices of the peoples of worldwide were presented.

11.1. *Ritual, Cults and Shamanism*

Sixty-three papers (58 English and 5 others) were related to deity worship, observances of ritual and ceremony and invocation of supernatural beliefs. The major societies considered were the Hindus, Piaroa Indians of Venezuela, peasants of Mexico, Brazil, Afghanistan, Israel, India, Korea, Ghana, Nigeria, Balkans and some African, Indians of Western United States. Some papers were on the nature of cult of deal and aspects of Shamanism.

11.2. *Ancestors*

Thirteen papers were on attitudes directed toward the deceased with especial references to the Far East and African Societies, some major topics were ancestor worship in Far Eastern rural urban societies and African tribal.

12. Psychological and Cognitive Anthropology

Four sessions were organized on the theme related to culture and personality studies. A total of 59 papers were presented in these sessions.

12.1. *Culture and Personality Anthropology*

There were 40 papers presented in this session. The main focus of the papers was on how to explore the relationship between model personality and culture, and the relationship between changes in social and cultural system and changes in the model personality. Some of these papers were based on the field work done in India, West Indies, Afghanistan, Mediterranean Island, New Guinea, Guatemala, Switzerland, New Zealand, and Guyanese societies.

12.2. *Adolescence*

Eight papers were related to the studies on cross-cultural adolescence. Some of these papers reviewed the recent works on adolescent growth and development contributed by physical anthropologists and other experts of human development. A few studies were on changing patterns of socialization related to adolescence and the stated case-studies were drawn from Indies, Hungary, Indonesia and Papua and New Guinea.

12.3. *Experience forms : their cultural and individual place and function*

Experience forms as fullest psychological happenings and their relation to conveying means to their culture were discussed in four papers in a separate session on 'Experience Forms.'

12.4. *Psychic Unity, Inference-making and Enculturation*

Seven papers were on Cognitive Anthropology. These papers discussed the arguments and evidences concerning hypothesis about the universality of discourse structures.

13. Language and Linguistic Anthropology

There were four sessions in the field of Linguistics in which 125 papers (107 English and 18 others) were related to the studies of languages. The following are the details of these sessions.

13.1. *Language and Man*

Twenty-four papers were on language capacity and acquisition as paradigmentican for man as a species. Vocallinguistic behaviour as continuity between animal and human communication, psychocio-linguistics, signs and symbols, linguistic and kinesic and language in face to face interactions were some principal topics covered in these papers.

13.2. *Languages and Thought*

Thiry-six papers (32 English and 4 others) were related to the theme of language and thought or semantic probabilities in human cognition and symbology. Some of these papers were based on the field-studies completed among the peoples of Liberia, Venezuela, Tibet, Alaska, Nigeria, India, Japan and Rumania.

13.3. *Language Evolution*

Thirty-two papers (28 English and 4 others) explored the methods and models for studying languages and changes in the language. Some of the topics covered by these papers were socio-economic factors in language split, the revival of Hebrew, historical linguistics, monolinguals and bilinguals, etc. The languages of the societies reported in various case-studies were those of the Soviet Union, English, Eskimo, New Guinea, South American societies such as the Nayan and the Yanomama Curl peoples of North Central India.

13.4. *Language in Many Ways*

In this session 33 papers (32 English and 1 other) were presented. These were related to language behaviour of individuals and groups; problems of description, verificability, interpretation and theoretical import. The societies and peoples from which the data were collected were the Andean, the Africans, the Taiwanians, the Americans, the Russians, the South Asian, including Indians, the Japanese, the Chinese and Mexicans.

14. Population Anthropology

Fifty papers presented in five sessions were related to

Population Anthropology. The following are the details of these sessions :

14.1. *Population and Social Organization*

The central focus of the 13 papers was establishing the relationship of various processes of population change and aspects of social organization. Some major topics covered were : marriage and group size, family planning and social communication, differential fertility and fecundity, and migration. The related case-studies were collected from Indonesia, Czechoslovakia, Nigeria, India, Pakistan and some American Indians of the USA.

14.2. *Population and Adaptation in Human Evolution*

Contributors of nine papers examined population dynamics from ecological and historical points of view. Human ecology, social evolution, population pressure and economy, etc. were some major topics discussed in these papers.

14.3. *The Status of the Female : Reproduction*

Thirteen papers were related to the studies of the general status of the female of various cultures and the lack of the anthropological data to report on this sector of the population. Some of the major topical areas examined were : lactation, residence patterns during the prenatal period, effects of harmones on female behaviour, pregnancy and nutrition, and midwifery.

The related case-studies included in these papers were collected from West Africa, West Indies, Yugoslavia, Switzerland, Ethiopia, Venezuela, Equador, the USA and India.

14.4. *Migration and Ethnicity*

Migration is one of the major aspects of the population. In one session devoted on the studies of migration, 15 papers were presented. Some of these papers examined cultural factors contributed to the assimilation of migrants and to the loss of ethnic identity in a new environment. These papers were based on the field work completed in Brazil, Switzerland, Papua, New Guinea, South Africa, the USA, Israel, Mexico, Argentina, Malaysia, UK, West Indies, Ghana and Equador.

15. Ethnicity

Five sessions were organized on the theme of ethnicity and 85 papers were presented there. A brief note on these sessions is as follows :

15.1. *Ethnicity and Competition for Resources*

Seven papers were related to the competition among the ethnic groups for their accumulation of resources. The underlying theme of these papers was oriented to the question of how group conflict and competition are structured by various peoples in different techno-environments. The related case-studies were drawn from simple and complex societies of Guyana, Nigeria, Peru, Equador and the United States.

15.2. *Interethnic relations, Boundary maintenance and conflict*

Twenty-three papers were on theory and method in the study of ethnicity, the learning and perception of ethnic identities, boundary maintenance and conflict, and ethnicity and its relationship to the competition for resources. Some of these papers were the product of the field work done in parts of European regions, *e.g.* Hungary, India, the USSR, North and South America.

15.3. *Ethnicity in the Americas*

Twenty-four papers were on the nature of race and ethnicity of Americas. Some of these papers discussed problems (3) raised by the presence of racial and ethnic minorities in Canada and the Caribbean, while other papers were based on the American experience.

15.4. *Mutual interaction of people and their built environment : A cross-cultural perspective*

Sixteen papers (15 English and 1 other) were devoted on the problem as what characteristics of people should be considered in environmental design and in the study of non-environment relations; what effects environment has on people; and the mechanisms which link people with environments. The related case-studies were drawn from tribal/non-tribal populations of New Zealand, Afghanistan, South-West Nigeria, Japan and Egypt.

15.5. *Organization of Behaviour in Face to Face interaction*

Fifteen papers were related to the organization of social interaction from cultural, social, and psychological perspectives through discussions of the inter-relationships between speech and gesture, facial expressions, posture and spacing. Some of these papers were based on the studies done in Japan, the USA, Mexico and Israel.

16. Cultural Dynamics

One hundred and Sixty-six papers (151 English and 15 others) were related to the aspects of cultural dynamics. These papers were presented in 14 sessions organized on various aspects of cultural and social change. The following is a brief account of these sessions :

16.1. *Multilateral Approaches to Social Change*

Twelve papers dealt with the various approaches of social change. Many times in socio-economic development programmes, communications are inadequate. Then the problem before Anthropology is how to improve the situation. The papers presented in this session were related to this question. The related case-studies of these papers were collected from West Indies, Mexico, South-East Asia and India.

16.2. *The Process of Urbanism*

Nine papers (8 English and 1 other) examined four aspects of urban studies. The relevance of Archaeology to urban planning, Ecology and urban environment, social organisation and the role of industry and technology in the urban process.

16.3. *Urbanization Process in America*

Seven papers (5 English and 2 others) were on the urbanization process in America. Of these, six papers were based on the field work done in parts of Latin America.

16.4. *American Indian Economic Development*

No paper seems to have been presented under this session.

16.5. *Changing Identities in South Asia*

Thirty papers explored social and ideological determinants of identity exchanges and definitions of social units, *e.g.* tribe, caste, family and bureaucract in South Asia. While several of these papers were based on the field work done in parts of India, others were related to the life and culture of Bangladesh, Ceylon and Pakistan.

16.6. *Ethnic Identities in Modern South-east Asia : Problem of Comparison, Conflict, Tradition and Development*

Thirteen papers explored prospects for the cultures of South-East Asia's tribal population in light of developing national policies plus economic, demographic and related factors. The related case-studies were drawn from Malaysia, Thailand, Vietnam, Combodia, the Philippines and Indonesia.

16.7 *West African Culture Dynamics*

Twenty-two papers (20 English and 2 others) dealt with the consideration of long-term African cultural development from the view points of Archaeology, Ethnology and History. The related case-studies were drawn from West Africa, North Africa, Sierra Leone, Ghana and North-East Africa.

16.8. *A Century of Change in East and Central Africa*

Fifteen papers (14 English and 1 other) were related to the changing patterns of economic, political and ethnic organization in contemporary East and Central Africa.

16.9. *Impact of Agrarian Reform on Local Indigenous Communities*

Eight papers (6 English and 2 others) dealt with the effects of agrarian reform on the economic, social and ideological structure of local tribal communities by social scientists and tribals. The related case-studies were drawn from West Indies, Mexico, Bolivia, Venezuela, and India.

16.10. *Fates of Indigenous Peoples*

Twelve papers (11 English and 1 other) were devoted to cross-cultural overview of the problems o findigenous peoples in the past and present, and prospects for the future. The related case-studies were drawn from Brazil, Venezuela, Peru, Canada, Africa and Mexico.

16.11. *Cooperatives, Collectives and Nationalized Industry as Modes of Popular Participation in National Development*

Eighteen papers (12 English and 6 others) were related to the problems and prospects rising out of the experience with cooperatives, etc. and other experiments in restructuring productive enterprises. The related case-studies were selected from the studies done in Africa, Israel, Bolivia, Bangladesh, the Sicilian Islands and Argentina.

16.12. *Interethnic Relations Boundary Maintenance and Conflict*

Twenty-three papers were related to the theory and

method of ethnicity, the learning and perception of ethnic identities, identity maintenance and boundary crossing. A few papers also discussed ethnicity and its relationship to the competition for resources.

17. Anthropological Study of Education

Twelve papers (11 English and 1 other) were presented on cultural and social approaches to the study of Education. Some of the main topics included in these papers were : Education and cultural transmission, comparative Education and social situations, Education and cultural pluralism and informal systems of Education. While a few papers were mainly theoretical in nature others were case-studies and descriptive. The latter included societies of Latin America, South and South-East Asia, the USA and Europe.

18. Cross-cultural Perspectives on the Women's Movement

Thirteen papers (12 English and 1 other) were devoted to the study of a cross-cultural comparison of women's movements and a consideration of cultures where there is no apparent women's movement or where there is resistance to women's liberation. The areas represented and considered were Africa, South and South-East Asia, the Middle East, Latin America, the West Indies, Europe and the USA.

19. The Status of the Female : Domestic and Public Power

Two papers were devoted to the means of determining the political status of women in society.

20. The Status of the Female : Social Trends

Thirteen papers (12 English and 1 other) were related to the status of female in the contemporary societies of Latin America, Africa, West Indies, India and South-East Asia. These papers discussed some major issues like what are the current patterns of behaviour of women ? What part of those patterns are being reported by anthropologists and others? How can we improve our viewing of female behaviour?

21. War : Its Causes and Correlates

The subject matter of 31 papers was related to the causes and correlates of warfare. The areas and societies represented and discussed were the Ojihwa, the Tonga Islands, the Alaskarn, Bushman of Kalabani, the Yaman Indians of the South-West North America, the Angkor of New Guinea, South America, Israel, and the Jiraro Indians of the Equadorian and Peruvian Montana.

22. The Future of the Human Species

Five papers (4 English and 1 other) were discussed on the future of the mankind. The related case-studies were drawn from the presents of Bangladesh, Ceylon and Papua and New Guinea.

23. Current Problems of the Profession in Historical perspective

Eight papers (7 English and 1 other) were on the problem of the Anthropology as a profession.

24. The Politics of Anthropology

How Anthropology has been related to the colonial interests of its practitioners, and how it promulgates and reflects the popular underlying assumptions about the nature of society was the subject matter of 15 papers presented in the session on the politics of Anthropology.

25. Naturalistic Explanations of Cultural Adaptation

Nineteen papers dealt with different problems of naturalistic explanation in Anthropology, viz. "How does a people come to have and continue to maintain certain characteristic adaptive mechanism."

26. Family Structure of Black America

Nine papers were related to the aspects of black American communities of the United States. These papers were concerned with family, law, education, economic development and social welfare of the black communities of the contemporary North America.

27. Fray Bartlome de Las Casas

In this session six papers (4 Fnglish and 2 others) were presented and a discussion followed on the condition of the Indians in contemporary Spanish America. The session, it may be noted here, was organized in cooperation with the Patronato Fray Bartolome de Las Casas of Chiapas (Mexico).

Other Activities

In addition to the academic sessions a large number of other events were scheduled, perhaps most impressive the world premiere of *Tamu-Tamu*, an opera commissioned by the Congress and composed by Gian Carlo Menotti. The opera was not exactly a commercial success, partly due to a very tight production schedule and partly due to some critics confusing Indonesia, the setting for the piece, with Indo-China only establishing the great tasks ahead for Anthropology in educating so many communities, including parts of the developed ones, about a larger culture of mankind. The opera emphasized the challenges involved in cross-cultural understanding and has since successfully been produced elsewhere.

The Congress' involvement in performing arts brought much favourable publicity and some temporary prominence for anthropology in the national media.

An American Folk Concert surprised foreign visitors with the strength of folk traditions in America.

A tour of three major archaeological sites in Illinois was organized and, along with other exhibits relating to the Ninth Congress, The Georgia Mobile Archaeology Lab was open for inspection.

A Native American group held a large Pow Wow on

Friday night, providing a demonstration of traditional dance and music for Congress delegates. Finally a large book fair was arranged.

The Youth for Mankind conference was a unique event, organized in conjunction with the Congress. This international gathering of high school students was beautifully organized of, by and for high school students with only a minimum of outside assistance.

Discussion Sessions

During the Chicago Congress a number of sessions were organized in which no final presentation of papers was made. Instead, they were kept for open discussion by the participants. The following is the list of these sessions :

1. New approaches to Development in Bilingual, Bicultural Communities
2. Anthropological Participation in the World Population Year
3. Alcohol Studies and Anthropology
4. Social Change in Socialist Societies
5. Patterns of European History
6. Language in Anthropology
7. American Indian Economic Development
8. Anthropology Today and Tomorrow
9. International Cooperation in Research and Documentation
10. Concept of Mankind
11. Youth for Mankind

Pre-and Post-Congress Conferences

As stated earlier, one of the remarkable features of the Chicago Congress was that many Pre-and Post-Congress Conferences were arranged at various institutions of the United States. The following is the complete list of these conferences held before and after the main congress meetings :

List of Pre-Congress Conferences

1. Origin of Agriculture (Woodstock conference center)
2. Problems and Possibilities of a Marxist Ethnology (University of Chicago)
3. Multilateral Approaches to Social Change (University of Wisconsin-Oshkosh)
4. Urbanization Processes in America (University of Wisconsin-Oshkosh)
5. The Processes of Urbanism (five St. Louis-area schools)
6. Migration and Ethnicity (University of Wisconsin-Oshkosh)
7. New Approaches to Development in Bilingual, Bicultural Communities
8. Population and Social Organisation (University of Wisconsin-Oshkosh)
9. Population and Adaptation in Human Evolution (University of Wisconsin-Oshkosh)
10. Cross-Cultural Perspectives on Cannabis (University of Chicago)
11. Alcohol Studies and Anthropology (University of Chicago)
12. Early Palaeolithics of East Africa (McGill University, Montreal)
13. Affective Response in Man (North-western University, Chicago)
14. Affective Response in Man (North-western University and American Hospital Association)
15. Structure of Oral Literature (North-western University, Chicago)
16. Folklore in the Modern World (Indiana University, Bloomington)
17. War : Its Causes and Correlates (Notre Dame University, Indiana)
18. Organization of Behaviour in Face to Face Interaction (University of Chicago)
19. Mutual Interaction of People (University of Wisconsin-Milwaukee and the Johnson Foundation)
20. Changing Identities in South Asia (Michigan State University, Michigan)

21. Dental Anthropology (University of Chicago)
22. Dermatoglyphics (Trent University, Ontario)
23. Medical Anthropology
24. Northern Atlantic Maritime European (University of Wisconsin-Oshkosh)
25. Bibliography and Documentation (University of Chicago)
26. Anthropological study of Education (University of Wisconsin-Oshkosh)
27. International Conference on Adolescence (University of Wisconsin-Oshkosh)
28. Cooperatives, collectives and Nationalized industry (University of Wisconsin-Oshkosh)
29. Impact of Agrarian Reform (University of Wisconsin-Oshkosh)
30. Ethnicity in Americans (University of Wisconsin-Oshkosh)
31. Psychic Unity, Inference making and Enculturation (University of Wisconsin-Milwaukee and the Johnson Foundation)
32. Fi-social Interrelations in Population Adaptation (Wayne State University)
33. The Future of the Human Species (University of Wisconsin-Oshkosh)

Post-Congress Conferences

1. Primates : Chromosomes and Evolution (Wayne State University Detroit)
2. Visual Anthropology (University of Illinois Chicago (August 28-31.)

Sessions that Originated Earlier in the form of Symposium

1. Origins of African Plant Domestication (Burg Wartenstein, 1972)
2. Palaeoanthropology : Behaviour (Burg Wartenstein)
3. Ethnological Museology (UNESCO's International Council of Museums, Milwaisree Museum).

The Permanent Council and General Assembly

The Permanent Council held two meetings to conduct the business of the IUAES. It discussed ways and means to raise funds to multiply the academic activities of the IUAES. It also received three invitations to hold the next Congress in Canada, France and India and voted for India.

It was also decided to hold the next meeting of Permanent Council at Rome in 1976. In addition to the nomination of the national delegations (*see* Appendix II), the Permanent Council elected the President of the Tenth ICAES and the IUAES (Prof. L.P. Vidyarthi, India). The other officers of the IUAES were also elected and later ratified by the General Assembly. The following were the office-bearers of the IUAES, elected at Chicago for a period of five years (1973-78) :

PRESIDENT

L.P. Vidyarthi, India

POST-PRESIDENT

Sol Tax, USA

VICE-PRESIDENTS

C. von Furer-Haimendorf, London
Robert Gessain, France
Chi Nakane, Japan
I. Nazimiro, Nigeria
Lise Schwidetzky, Germany
V.P. Yakimov, USSR

SECRETARIAT

Cyril Belshaw, Canada
Y.V. Bromley, USSR
Elizabeth Colson, USA
Jeen Cusinier, France
V.P. Grottanetti, Italy
L. Hamamzy, UAR
I.P. Singh, India
D.P. Sinha, India
Hisashsuzuki, Japan
J.S. Weiner, London.

Publications

On the occasion of the Ninth International Congress of Anthropological and Ethnological Session each participant was provided with a pull out file containing the details of the working sessions scheduled to be held at appropriate place and time. This file contained abstracts of all the papers (over 1,600) received by the organizing committee till June 1973. It has already been noted earlier that the Ninth International Congress was planned from the beginning not only to include as many of the scholars from every part of the world as possible, but also with a view to the eventual publication of the papers. Since 1974, Moutan of the Neatherlands (an internationally known publisher) has been publishing the proceedings of the Congress in over 50 volumes.

As of September 1975, the following volumes have appeared in print under the General editorship of Prof. Sol Tax, Prof. of Anthropology, Chicago University, and the President of the Ninth ICAES :

1. *African Dilemma Tales* (172 pp)
2. *After the Australopithecines* (2 Vols. 984 pp)
3. *Approaches to Maritime Anthropology* (336 pp)
4. *Ethnicity and Resource Competition in Plural Societies* (232 pp)
5. *Migration : Models and Adaptive Strategies* (320 pp)
6. *Prehistoric Maritime Adaptations of the Circumpolar Zone* (416 pp)
7. *Principles of Visual Anthropology* (544 pp)
8. *Topics and Utopias in Health* (560 pp)
9. *Organization of Behaviour in Face to Face Interaction* (528 pp)
10. *Population and Social Organization* (376 pp)
11. *Women Cross-Culturally* (588 pp)
12. *War : Its Causes and Correlates* (2 Vols. 848 pp)
13. *Population and Social Organization* (376 pp)
14. *Being Female : Reproduction, Power, and Change* (264 pp)
15. *Cannabis and Culture* (568 pp)
16. *Migration Change and Development : Implications for Ethnic Identity and Political Conflict* (232 pp)

17. *Lithic Technology: Making and Using Stone Tools* (244 pp)
18. *Essays in the History of Anthropology* (240 pp)
19. *Primate Functional Morphology and Evolution* (448 pp)
20. *Palaeoanthropology* (608 pp)
21. *Socio-Ecology and Psychology of Primates* (512 pp)
22. *Biosocial Interrelations in Populalion Adaptation* (432 pp)
23. *Psychological Anthropology* (2 Vols. 992 pp)
24. *A Century of Change in Eastern Africa*
25. *Gastronomy : The Anthropology of Food and Food Habits*
26. *Rituals, Cults, Shamanism: The Realm of the Extra-Human* (2 Vols)
27. *Advances in Andean Archaeology*
28. *Cultural Continuity in Mesomerica*
29. *The Anthropological Study of Education*
30. *The Visual Arts : Plastic and Graphic*
31. *The Mutual Interaction of People and their Built Environment : A Cross-Cultural Perspective*
32. *Origins of Agriculture*
33. *The Anthropology of Clothing and Adornment*
34. *Anthropology and Mental Health : Setting a New Course*
35. *Oro-Facial Growth and Development*
36. *Youth in a Changing World : Cross-Cultural Perspectives on Adolescence*
37. *Discussion on War and Human Aggression*
38. *Medical Anthropology*
39. *Origins of African Plant Domestication*
40. *Early Palaeolithic in South and East Asia : Regional Manifestations and a Broader Perspective*
41. *Patterns in Oral Literature*
42. *Urbanization in the Americas from Its Beginning to the Present* (2 Vols.)
43. *Language and Man : Anthropological Issues*
44. *Language and Thought : Anthropological Issues*
45. *Popular Participation in Social Change : Cooperatives, Collectives, and Nationalized Industry* (2 Vols.)
46. *Development from Below : Anthropologists and Development Situations*

Press Coverage

The Ninth Congress was not only a major scientific meeting, but an important news event. Many of the sessions dealt with national or international social problems which were clearly worth attention. The various media and the news available were brought together by a vigorous campaign of publicity and cooperation with the needs of the media. There was extensive local coverage over all local media and stories in the Chicago newspapers were picked up by the wire services. As a consequence, discussions on alcoholism, cannabis, how there came to be Bromleys in Russia and the worldwide distribution of wealth were spread from Los Angeles to Houston and New York. Anthropology was presented in an almost uniformly favourable light as a "dynamic and viable field which was actively involved in researching and solving many of the world's major social problems." The media were so enthusiastic that the press facilities had to be radically expanded, and some anthropologists protected from too many interviews.

Part Five

THE THIRD WORLD ORIENTATION

10

The India—Delhi Congress : 1978

Soon after its return, the Indian delegates announced the acceptance of India's invitation to hold the Tenth ICAES at Delhi and other parts of the country which was very well received. The national delegation, consisting of Prof. L.P. Vidyarthi (Ranchi), Dr. Surajit C. Sinha (Calcutta), Dr. B.N. Sahay (New Delhi), Dr. K.S. Mathur (Lucknow), Dr. D.P. Sinha (Calcutta), Dr. Gopala Sarana (Dharwar) and Dr. I.P. Singh (New Delhi), held its first meeting on 15 March 1974 and took the decision to expand the delegation into an Organizing Committee by including other eminent scholars from different parts of the country. In the meantime it was decided that the President would issue Newsletters half-yearly to report the progress regarding the Congress.

The Organizing Committee held its first meeting in the hall of the Indian Institute of Public Administration on 11 November 1975, and finalised the details to be placed in the Permanent Council at Rome.

The Organizing Committee took major decisions and fixed up the dates of the Congress at Delhi from 10 to 16 December. It also decided to hold the post-Congress Sessions at important institutions in different parts of the country. The selection of the major theme of the Congress was of special debate. Keeping the problem of the Third World Countries in focus and the need for striking a balance between man and environment, it was decided that the major theme should be : Anthropology and the Challenges of Development.

A 16-page printed document embodying the outline for the forthcoming Congress was placed at the Rome meeting on 3-5 May 1976. The proposal was well received and found full support from all the delegations present there. The general impression of the Permanent Council regarding the Congress planning was conveyed to the leader of the national delegation by the IUAES Secretary General Prof. Lawrence Krader in the following words :

> The meeting of the Permanent Council at Rome, May 1976, may be accounted a success, particularly in view of the positive reception of the proposals of Indian Delegation to the IUAES, so ably represented by yourself. The future of the ICAES, being therefore assured, we may confidently assume that the Tenth ICAES will rank among the strongest in the history of our International Union and Congress. This prediction is made not least in view of the support given to the ICAES by the Government and the academic community of your country. The energy and astuteness with which you have marshalled the support for undertaking under your direction have given course for considerable satisfaction both among the Permanent Council and the Executive Board of the IUAES.

With the passage of time the preparation for the Congress gained momentum. An office was established in Delhi in February 1978 and Dr. Binod C. Agrawal (Ahmedabad) was nominated as the Executive Secretary. He, along with his team, set the Congress secretariat which was later joined by Dr. R.K. Gulati and Dr. B.R. Ghosh, two senior officers of the Anthropological Survey of India. As provided in the IUAES Constitution, in my capacity as the President, I nominated Prof. I.P. Singh as Secretary-General of the Delhi Congress.

In response to my several Newsletters published in the leading anthropological journals of the world and my trips to Canada, the USA, USSR and European countries as well as our discussions in the meetings of the Indian Science Congress at Waltair (1975), Delhi (1976), Bhubaneshwar (1977) and

Ahmedabad (1978), the annual meetings of the Indian Anthropological Associations and finally discussions in the meetings of programmes Committee, a detailed programme of symposia, sessions, workshops, etc. were finalised and their Chairpersons and co-Chairpersons were nominated.

Subject to certain modifications the Scientific programmes of the Congress will include the following symposia, sessions, general lectures, commission meetings, etc. :

A. Physical Anthropology

1. Morphology
2. Physical adaptation
3. Biological cariation
4. Evolution, human welfare and society
5. Comparative primate Biology
6. Biology and behaviour
7. Nutrition, growth and development
8. Bio-chemical genetics
9. Physical Anthropology and sports
10. Human Cytogenetics
11. Forensic Anthropology
12. Applied Physical Anthropology
13. The Dermatoglyphics
14. Genetic Counselling
15. Ethnogenesis and other invited lectures

B. Social and Cultural Anthropology

1. The Ethnography of invocations and incantations : Verbal symbolism and ritual structure
2. Political Anthropology
3. Economic Anthropology
4. Anthropology of Music
5. Anthropology of traditional performances
6. Anthropology of social movements
7. Psychological Anthropology
8. Concept of a tribe
9. Social Demography
10. Anthropology of food

11. Scriptural literature in cultural contexts
12. Anthropological bibliography and documentation

C. Prehistory

1. Lower palaeolithic
2. Middle palaeolithic
3. Upper palaeolithic
4. Mesolithic
5. Neolithic-chalcolithic
6. Bronze and Iron Age
7. Prehistoric technology
8. Indus script and invited lectures

D. Anthropological Linguistics

1. Munda language
2. Sino-Tibetan languages
3. Theoretical foundations of linguistics
4. English in the Third World
5. Problems and methods of mapping language change and invited lectures

SYMPOSIA

A. Physical Anthropology

1. Man, Ecology and population
2. Biology and Culture

B. General and Social Anthropology

1. Anthropology of highlands
2. Ethnicity and ethnic awareness among overseas Indian communities
3. Ideas and Trends in World Anthropology
4. The process of ethnic integration : Some theoretical methodological problems
5. Neo-evolutionism and Marxism

6 Kinship system
7. Problems of urbanization in the Third Word : An anthropological perspective
8. Nomadism
9. Visual Anthropology
10. Symposium of biological reproduction and its correlation with pattern of economic production
11. Socio-cultural variables in work organization in developing countries

. Prehistory

1. Tertiary and quaternary climatic changes in arid and semi-arid zones
2. Origins of urbanization in south and east Asia

D. Anthropological Linguistics

1. Ethnography of communication
2. Language, planning and national development
3. Ethnicity, identity and language
4. Literacy and language use

The Post-Congress

The main Congress (December 10-16) will be followed by a series of post-congresses (December 18-20) at certain selected centres of specialization in various parts of India. For the present, proposals for holding such post-congresses had been received from the following places :

	Place	*Themes*
1.	*Bhubaneshwar :*	Anthropology of shifting cultivation
2.	*Bombay* :	Population structure and human variation
3.	*Calcutta* :	Folklore and Literary Anthropology
4.	*Calcutta* :	Applied and Action Anthropology
5.	*Chandigarh* :	Human origins
6	*Delhi* :	Primitive Economic formation

	Place	Themes
7.	*Delhi* :	Problems and methods of mapping in Ethnography and Anthropology
8.	*Delhi* :	Biometrical approach to Physical Anthropology
9.	*Delhi* :	Social invisibility of women in Anthropology
10.	*Hyderabad* :	Hunger, work and quality of life
11.	*Lucknow* :	Social Anthropology of peasantry
12.	*Madras* :	Religion and Social Change
13.	*Mysore* :	Linguistic Anthropology
14.	*Mysore* :	Problems of Multilingualism: Language use in Education, administration and mass communication
15.	*Poona* :	Medical Anthropology
16.	*Poona* :	Recent advances in Indo-Pacific prehistory
17.	*Port Blair* :	Island culture
18.	*Ranchi* :	Primitive World and its Transformations : Life styles, world views and values

The IUAES Activities

The IUAES has been comparatively quite active during this period under review (August 1973—December 1978). The following 11 commissions have been in action though some of them have developed elaborate programmes and had some meetings while others have postponed their work to be undertaken during the Congress.

	COMMISSIONS	CHAIRPERSONS
1.	*Population* :	Dr. Moni Nag, New York
2.	*Urgent Anthropology* :	Prof. Anna Hohenwart G. Vienna
3.	*Homicide and Genocide* :	Prof. Cyril Belshaw, Vancouver
4.	*Futurology* :	Prof. B.K. Roy Burman, Shanti Niketan
5.	*Documentation* :	Dr. L.P. Vidyarthi, Ranchi
6.	*Women* :	Dr. Leela Dube, Delhi

COMMISSIONS	CHAIRPERSONS
7. *Museum* :	Prof. P.H. Pott Leiden and Dr M.K. Gautam
8. *Visual Anthropology* :	Prof. M. Oka, Tokyo and Dr. K.N. Sahay
9. *Man & Environment* :	Prof. Milton M.R. Freeman, Hamilton, Canada
10. *Nomadism* :	Dr. Philip Carl Salzman, Montreal
11. *Food* :	Prof. R.S. Khare, Virginia

The Executive Committee of the IUAES held four meetings at regular intervals at Chicago (8 September 1973), Paris (10-11 December 1975), Rome (3-5 May 1976) and London (25-26 October 1977). In these meetings many significant decisions were taken to intensify the academic programmes established collaborations with INGOS and improve the financial position of the IUAES. The initiative and active roles of Prof. Cyril Belshaw in his capacity as the Chairman of the Finance Committee as well as Programmes Committee deserve special mention.

The recognition of *Current Anthropology*, the world journal of Anthropology, as the official organ of IUAES has been a matter of considerable significance in the history of World Anthropology. It has further opened up new areas of collaboration with the editors of anthropological journals all over the world.

The proposed amendments to the Constitution, for which grand work has been prepared and which will be adopted during the Delhi conference, will further revitalize the Union in terms of its structure and function.

We eagerly look forward to successful sessions both of the Congress and of the Union, and we sincerely hope that these will be very different from the earlier Congresses, for it will be the first ever Congress to be held in a Third World Country.

11

Conclusion

Though Anthropology took a definite shape as a discipline in the mid-nineteenth century, it took almost a hundred years to establish a professional organization at the international level. As the formative phase of Anthropology has remained linked with the exploration of life and culture of colonial countries, and as the British scholars were ahead in this endeavour, they took the lead in this field. In the fitness of their roles and preparedness, they convened the first international Congress of Anthropological and Ethnological Sciences in London in 1934. From the proceedings of this first Congress it is also quite evident that the Royal lords associated with colonial expansion were deeply involved in its organization. From the inaugural speech of the Duke of York, the support in organizing the first Congress is evident as well as their representation in the organizing committee are clear indications of their pronounced interest in supporting the organization of the first World Congress.

In terms of academic contents, the Congress appeared to be more concerned with Anatomy and Physical Anthropology (94), Ethnography of colonial countries (90), technology (21), language and writing (23). The discipline of Anthropology during that Congress also included sessions on Sociology (34) and Psychology (21) in a big way. The impact of British Anthropology continued to dominate in the successive three Congresses held at Copenhagen (1938), Brussels (1948) and

Vienna (1952). Both Physical Anthropology and Ethnology continued to figure prominently almost on equal basis. The in-roads of the new areas of research were almost negligible, though in the Vienna Congress, which was held after the ravages of the second World War, more emphasis was given on urgent researches of the primitive pockets and extremely backward tribes of the world.

It was after about a quarter of a century that the Congress left its place of origin (i.e. Europe), crossed the Atlantic and met in Philadelphia in 1956. This Congress held for the first time in the new hemisphere was evidently significant in the light of the preparedness that the American Anthropology had made after the second World War.

The Philadelphia Congress, again, has to be viewed as the first important anthropological conference organized by Wenner Gren Foundation for Anthropological Research Inc. in New York in 1952 under the dynamic Chairmanship of A.L. Kroeber which resulted in the publication of *Anthropology Today* (A.L. Kroeber, 1953) and *An Appraisal of Anthropology Today* (Sol Tax *et al.*, 1956). In general, these two volumes goes to define and defend the status of Anthropology "as a co-ordinating holistic and integrative science, as special bodies of international knowledge about man, flowing out of man, centred in him and product of him."

Moreover, this period, characterized with the liberation of several colonial countries and their increasing contact with America, gave birth to the trends of Americanisation of Anthropology.

Again, during this Congress, the process of internationalization became more prcnounced also because, for the first time, a strong Soviet delegation attended the Congress and emphasized the application of the theory of neo-evolutionism and Marxism for a correct understanding of the social situations, particularly in the newly liberated colonial countries of Africa, Asia and Latin America. Such a participation of scholars from the two ideologically divided worlds emphasizing varied theoretical, methodological and substantive materials generated balancing influence on the deliberations.

After Philadelphia, the world Anthropological Congress again crossed the Atlantic and met in Paris in 1960. Though this Congress was marked with the dominance of French language and style in the deliberations and planning of the conference, the academic contents remained more or less on the pattern of Philadelphia Congress. The French structural school, however, found pronounced prominence partly because of its old tradition in France and partly because of the emergence and recognition of Levi-Strauss as a prominent scholar of this school. The participation of Soviet scholars continued, though because of varied linguistic barriers, the inter-actions among scholars remained restricted.

The internationalization of this discipline, however, took a new turn when this Congress was held, for the first time, in a Socialist country (Moscow,1964) when the national scholarship was once again over-emphasized, and overwhelmingly represented. This Congress, however, brought recognition to the European and American neo-evolutionists, especially Leslie A. White, who had so far remained considerably ignored in his homeland. The scholars from the newly liberated countries also found better recognition and representation. In general, again, it was for the first time that the Soviet scholarship and institutions were exposed to first-hand contacts and inter-actions with the rest of the world. It evidently gave a new recognition to Soviet Anthropology and Ethnography, and aided increased incentive and impetus to liberal expansion of the discipline in the USSR.

With the organization of Eighth Congress at Tokyo-Kyoto in 1968, the internationalization of the anthropological congress was better realised when it was held for the first time in an Asian country. It was the second effort of the Japanese to host an international event, the first being the Pacific Science Congress held in 1966. In view of the language difficulty a few western scholars were invited to help the Organizing Committee. In addition to rich academic programmes covering the various branches of Anthropology, there was considerable emphasis on Japanese Anthropology, Sociology, History, etc.

It was for the first time that the community of World Anthropologists were exposed to the Japanese hospitality, good will and wider variety of national scholarship. It was realized that though it is deeply rooted to its own national language, Japanese Anthropology has been greatly exposed to both American and European influence.

Among several other international events, the memorable one was the get-to-gether of the large number of the associates of the Current Anthropology under the dynamic guidance of Prof. Sol Tax. Everybody left with the impression that Anthropology had its own worldwide journal, linking them with the rest of the world.

The next congress (1973), again, came back to the USA and was held in Chicago. The Congress planning was such that it attracted the largest crowd of anthropologists as well as the scientists of the allied discipline (about 4,500 persons). Almost every topic related to man and his works was discussed either in the pre-Congress, the plenary Congress or the post-Congress sessions. The participation and inter-action among the scholars were maximized with the arrangements of simultaneous translations in five languages (English, French, German, Spanish and Russian), and by holding all the plenary sessions as well as lodging all the delegates in the same hotel. This Congress was evidently different from other Congresses as large number of scholars from the Third World countries participated and presented their papers in the various sessions. This congress generated such a large number of papers (about 2,000) which are in the process of publication in more than 80 volumes under the major title, the *World Anthropology*.

Thus, "many who attended the Ninth Congress were convinced that Anthropology would not be the same in the future. The fact that the next Congress (India, 1978) will be our first in the Third World may be symbolic of the change."

The Delhi Congress evidently is different from the other world congresses. It gets reflected from the policy, planning and programmes that are before us. The Congress is not confined only to a hotel or a national capital city (Delhi) but has been planned to involve almost every important anthropological centre located in different parts of the country through organizing 19 post-congress sessions including one in the Andaman Islands. There is considerable emphasis on deliberations, discussions, commission meetings and promotion of scientific good will among fellow scientists drawn from all over the world.

Along with the Congress programmes, several international organizations, namely International Linguistic Association, International Dermatoglyphics Association, International Association of the Biologists, International Council of Museums, and the newly-established Association of the Editors of the Journals in Anthropology are holding their annual conferences. The IUAES sponsored project, 'Anthropology for the Future' under the chairpersonship of Sol Tax and this author makes a new promise for developing a comprehensive set of publication of books in the different branches of Anthropology, which should find universal acceptance, and which would be good enough to be translated in important languages of the world. This, evidently, is a revolutionary effort to internationalize Anthropology for which the seeds are being sown in a developing country.

At the organizational level, IUAES is also undergoing revolutionary changes. During the last five years, the Executive Committee along with its Programme and Finance Sub-Committees under the chairmanship of Cyril Belshaw have streamlined the activities of the Union. Under the guidance of IUAES President, the 10 commissions have been quite active. We are heading towards a series of amendments in the IUAES Statutes in Delhi, which will definitely make the Union more vigorous, democratic and active than what it has so far remained.

Thus, this preliminary and brief survey of the 10 Congresses held in last 44 years and related activities of the IUAES reflects the genesis and development of Anthropology as reflected through these Congresses. While it does not tell the whole story of the Congress, it does reflect how, with the passage of time, the two trends of internationalization as well as indigenization in Anthropology have got blended together. The contemporary status of Anthropology reflects a synthesis of the continued efforts of a large number of scholars drawn from different parts of the world, and from the different branches of Anthropology. These liberal and scientific efforts have enabled us to present a better understanding of man and his culture. The 'Anthropology for the Future' will still make the picture clearer for which we should keep ourselves scientifically active and alert.

The IUAES Historical Notes, 1962-1978

The International Union of Anthropological and Ethnological Sciences (IUAES), as it is constituted at present, is made up of two formerly independent and equal bodies, the IUAES which was its immediate forerunner, and the International Congress of Anthropological and Ethnological Sciences (ICAES). The ICAES was founded in 1934 on the initiative of a group of ethnologists, who held their first Congress in London in that year, and resolved to hold quadrennial congresses thereafter. They limited themselves to the activities of Human Biology, by which Anthropology in the limited sense was meant, and Ethnology, which included both Cultural and Social Anthropology. The primary, virtually the exclusive, purpose of their undertakings was to hold periodic meetings in different countries whereby formal scientific papers would be read, in conjunction with the development of formal and informal activities directly related to scientific research and publication in the several fields of the ICAES. A President, Vice-Presidents and a Scientific Secretary were elected who had responsibility for running the congresses, publishing the proceedings and taking up such matters as arose in the given state of the sciences at that time.

The quadrennial congresses held after London were at Copenhagen in 1938 (II ICAES), Brussels 1948 (III ICAES), Vienna 1952 (IV ICAES), Philadelphia 1956 (V ICAES), Paris 1960 (VI ICAES), Moscow 1964 (VII ICAES) and Tokyo 1968 (VIII ICAES). According to the Statutes that were in force at that time, the bodies responsible for the affairs of the ICAES was the Permanent Council, constituted of representatives

Contributed by Lawrence Krader

chosen from among the delegations to the ICAES, each according to the manner of the body of scientists in the different countries.

The IUAES was founded in 1948, on the occasion of the III ICAES, on the initiative of UNESCO, and had responsibility primarily for maintaining relations among the national bodies of anthropological and ethnological scientists, and between the ICAES and UNESCO. At the time of the foundation of the IUAES the most active figures were Paul Rivet, Henry Vallois, Pedro Bosch-Gimpera, Sergio Sergi, Robert Heine-Geldern, Daryll Forde, Meyer Fortes, I. Potekhin, G. Debets, M.J. Herskovits, A.V. Kidder II, and William Fenton. These had replaced an earlier group gathered around J.L. Myres, which had been instrumental in holding the first ICAES (at London). Although the ICAES and the IUAES were formally separate bodies during the period 1948-1964, the leading personnel tended to be the same in both because the latter was convened only on the occasion of the Congresses. In its organization, the Permanent Council varies slightly from this state of affairs, for it met both on the occasions of the Congresses and once during the inter-Congress period, and was concerned during this time chiefly with the affairs of the ICAES, concerning the place, time and programme of the Congresses. Pedro Bosch-Gimpera who was the leading figure in the formation of the IUAES and its Secretary-General from 1956 to 1964 was active at this time in developing contacts of the IUAES with the national organizations and with the UNESCO.

During the 1960s, two changes were introduced into both bodies, one formal and the other substantive. On the initiative of the UNESCO the periodicity of the meetings of the Congresses was changed from a four-year to a five-year cycle, a formal change. On the initiative of members of the ICAES and the IUAES during the Congress in Paris in 1960, and later in 1962, at the meeting of the Permanent Council in Prague, a working group was formed to constitute the ICAES and the IUAES as one body and accordingly to change the Statutes. The working group was formed by H. Vallois and P. Bosch-Gimpera, who thereupon drew on G. Olivier and L. Krader for the tasks of effecting the substantive change and causing the statutes to reflect this. The new organizational plan and the revised statutes were adopted de facto at the VII ICAES at Moscow in 1964, and de jure at the VIII ICAES at Tokyo in 1968. The initiative for the reorganization of the ICAES and the revision of the Statutes of both was taken, in the illness of S.P. Tolstov, the President of the ICAES at the occasion of the VII ICAES, by G.F. Debets, its Secretary. The initiative in the adoption of the definitive reorganization and of the statutory revisions was undertaken by Masao Oka, the President of the VIII ICAES at Tokyo in 1968.

Since the time of founding the IUAES, a quantum leap in the size of the ICAES has been taken. Compared to the participants in the Congresses held in the 1930s and 1940s, who numbered in the hundreds, the Congresses held thereafter have tended to include thousands of participants. The enormous organizational tasks of arranging meetings, both formal and informal, likewise living and transportation for the participants has fallen to the host country. The scientific public should be cognizant of the services of those who have been responsible for the Congresses. On the reorganization of the IUAES and the ICAES into one body, the organizational tasks did not diminish but increased in both scope and complexity. This was the result of the quantitative increase of scientific activity generally, and of the number of scientific organizations and of their organizational activities during the past two decades.

During this period, particularly under the incumbencies of Henri Vallois, S.P. Tolstov and Masao Oka, the ICAES organism was the concern of its President and the secretariat of the IUAES was the concern of the Secretary-General, whose task it was to maintain relations with the national organizations, associations and academic institutions on the one hand, and with the international non-governmental organizations on the other.

The relations of the IUAES with the UNESCO are in part direct, with reference to common tasks and programmes with the UNESCO Secretariat, and in part indirect. The direct relations with UNESCO have generated such documents as the UNESCO Statement on Race, in its several redactions. The IUAES has moreover provided expert advice in such areas of UNESCO activity as the Arid Zones Programme, and the Programme against illiteracy. The indirect relations of the IUAES with UNESCO are maintained primarily through two International Non-Governmental Organizations—the International Council of Philosophy and Humanistic Studies, and the International Social Science Council—the IUAES being represented on both. The IUAES moreover maintains formal relations with the International Council of Scientific Unions (ICSU) having participated in the International Biological Programme, which was organized by ICSU.

The Permanent Council, which has been responsible for running the affairs of the ICAES since its foundation, has since the conjunction of the IUAES with the ICAES, been responsible for running the affairs of both the bodies. Until the reorganization de facto at Moscow the Permanent Council meetings, both at the time of the congresses and at the inter-Congress meetings, had been devoted to organizational matters alone. Following the reorganization de facto at Moscow in 1964, it was resolved that scientific reports by the host country during the inter-Congress meetings of the Permanent Council be heard, in order that the national delegations learn something of the state of the sciences in the various parts of the world. The first of these meetings, combining organizational with scientific matters was held in London in 1966, the second in Copenhagen in 1971, and the third in Rome in 1976. On each occasion an outstanding address was made, by the late Maurice Freedman in London, by F. Barth in Copenhagen, and by Vinigi Grottanelli in Rome.

The reason for the reorganization of the ICAES and IUAES was primarily a matter of concern with the question of continuity. The ICAES as it was constituted in the past was dissolved with each Congress and reconstituted anew in a different country. The practices of the host country determined not the scientific programme, which was and remains the responsibility of the Permanent Council, but the fate of the scientific exhibits and displays, performances, and the dispositions of gifts of money, scientific objects and books fell to no one's responsibility. The establishment of the IUAES as the perpetual body of the IUAES and ICAES was the main desideratum and the main result of the reorganization. With the increasing scientific activities, a number of institutions have been organized which have gained international recognition in the past three decades. Among them the International Association of Human Biologists, the Societe Internationale des Etudes Folkloriques, and international bibliographic undertakings and institutions together with scientific publications such as *Current Anthropology* have worked with and through the IUAES in the interest of international anthropology and ethnology generally. The UNESCO in turn has communicated through the IUAES with these international organizations within the scientific disciplines.

The relations with the United Nations, during the past decade have been developed, in particular with reference to population studies and the studies of arid zones, the latter in continuity with an earlier relation with UNESCO in this field. The UN Economic and Social Council (UNECOSOC) has played the leading part in these undertakings of late and has enlisted the IUAES in this pursuit. These spheres of activity in relation to UNECOSOC are new in the IUAES and are still to be further developed.

When in 1964 Henri Vallois, Pedro Bosch-Gimpera, Robert Heine-Geldern and S.P. Tolstov asked me to take over the post of General Secretary, which had been filled until then by P. Bosch-Gimpera, it was with the understanding that a broad scope of activities was to be instituted. The development of the relations to the International Council of Museums (ICOM) are among the foremost of these. The Director of ICOM during the period 1964-1968 was Georges-Henri Reviere, who was active in developing a number of activities of ethnographic museums and museology in conjunction with the IUAES.

The guidance of the activities of the IUAES lies in the hands of the Permanent Council. Yet that body is large and its meetings costly; hence it is limited to two meetings every five years. The experience has been that more frequent meetings of the officers of the IUAES are necessary. In order to extend both national and disciplinary representation, a secretariat has been formed, which, together with the elected officers, has formed the Executive Committee of the IUAES. This executive body has held meetings in recent years no less than once a year, the meetings being dictated either by the urgency of the problems before it, or the occasion of meetings of other scientific bodies.

The policy in regard to financing and funding of the IUAES during the 1950s and 1960s was one of firmly regulated priorities, the highest of which was the financing of the activities of the ICAES; all other demands for funds were subordinated to this priority. The question of financing the Secretariat of the IUAES was raised in meetings of the Permanent Council held in Moscow in 1964, in London in 1966, and in Tokyo in 1968, when these priorities were maintained and affirmed. These are policies which closely conform to the traditions of both the IUAES and ICAES. They are opposed to the bureaucratization of science and permit such moneys as are raised to be expended for the purposes of scientific research and publication.

I close with some questions for future consideration :

(1) It might be well to reflect at this time on the present and future of the ICAES and the IUAES. The move of the ICAES for the first time to a Third World country is a matter of considerable gratification to the IUAES. The degree of sophistication in running the affairs of the IUAES has been enhanced. There has been a certain amount of concern with financing, but these have been in no way materially different from the nature of these activities in the past. There is therefore no reason to feel that the ICAES should be held in one part of the world as against another. Successful Congresses have been held in the east and the west, north and south. The future of the Congresses should therefore be decided on the merits of the individual offerings to play the host.

(2) The increase in the size of the Congresses has been a matter of some corcern. But the answer to this is simple. Since we are a democratically run organization, the size of the Congress, as measured by the number of the participants, will be decided by the participating scientists themselves. The organizers can do nothing but conform to the general desires. Yet if there are supervening difficulties, they are to be fully aired at the Permanent Council and General Assembly meetings. Having held a certain number of discussions about these matters, the result of these appears to be that the ICAES remains the chief priority of the IUAES, and will continue to absorb most of its

funds. The problems of organizing the Congresses anew are most complex, however, and perhaps it should be considered that a permanent staff member of the secretariat of the IUAES be responsible for joining with the organizers of the Congress in the host country and helping to transmit the experience of running the new one in the light of lessons learned from the old.

(3) The responsibility for running each Congress appears to remain that of the country which issues the invitation to hold the Congress and play the host to the anthropologists and ethnologists throughout the world. The continuation of this practice should be critically examined.

(4) The Permanent Council meetings have been the occasion, since 1966, for holding "mini-Congresses", the content of which is generally determined by the host delegation. Perhaps the themes and nature of these smaller undertakings should be put into some systematic order.

(5) In reference to the INGOs, the principal relations of the IUAES have been with the UNESCO and its relevant organs, the International Council for Philosophy and Humanistic Studies, the International Social Science Council, and the International Council of Scientific Unions. Without reflection on the importance of these relations, it nevertheless should be considered that relations to UNECOSOC and to the regional organizations of Asia and the Far East, Latin America and Africa should be developed. This requires close study of the general UN programmes and the specific regional programmes in order to determine where the IUAES has the most relevant contribution to make.

(6) The emphasis on the practical side of science emerges out of relations to governments INGOs and the like. This inhibits the theoretical and critical development of science. These matters should be carefully weighed.

(7) During my unduly long incumbency as Secretary General, the IUAES has been run with a minimum of bureaucratic structure, and has passed through a number of crises with a minimum of sound and fury.

APPENDIX II

Permanent Council (1973-78)

Argentinien

Prof. Dr. O. Menghin
Sociedad Argentina de Antropologia
Moreno 350
Buenos Aires, Argentina

Australia

Prof. C.H. Berndt
Department of Anthropology
The University of Western Australia
Nedlands, Western Australia

Austria

Prof. Mme. A. Hohenwart-Gerlachstein
Institut fur Volkerkunde der Universitat
UniversitatsstraBe 7
1010 Wien, Austria

Belgium

Mme. S. Vrydagh, Secretaire General
Societe Royale Belge d'Anthropologie
31, rue Vautier
Bruxelles 4, Belgium

Bolivia

Prof. Miranda G. Cordero
Museo Nacional de Arqueologia
Casilla Of. 64
La Paz, Bolivia

Brazil

Prof. Le Loureiro Fernandes, Director
Departmento de Pesquisas da Universidade do Parana
Rua General Carneiro 460; 60 andar.
Curitiba, Parana, Brazil

Bulgarien

Prof. Dr. P.N. Boev
Institut morphologii Ban
Poptomova 27
Sofia, Republique Populaire de Bulgarie

Canada

Dr. Cyril Belshaw, Chairman
University of British Columbia
Department of Sociology and Anthropology
Vancouver, British Columbia

Chile

Mme. Grete Mostny, Directora
Museo de Historia Natural
Casilla 787
Santiago, Chile

China

Dr. P'an Ch'un, Director
Bureau of Foreign Affairs of
the Academ a Sinion
Peking, China

Columbia

Dr. Gerardo Reichel-Dolmatoff, Jefe
Departamento de Antropologia de la Universidad de los Andes
Calle 18, carrera I-E
Apartado Aereo 4976
Bogota, D.F., Columbia

Cuba

Dr. A. Leon Perez
Instituto de Etnologia y Folklore de la
Acad. de Ciencias, Capitolio National
La Habana, Cuba

Eng. D. Peroz Franco, Director
Centro de Informacion Cientifica y Technica
Universidad de la Habana
Apartado 6022, La Habana Cuba

Dr. Rafael Lopez Valdes, Director
Academia de Ciencias de Cuba
Instituto de Etnologia
Palacio Aldama, Reina No. I Esq. A Amistad
La Habana—Cuba

Czechoslovakia

Dr. O. Skalnikova, Secretary
Czechoslovak Academy of Sciences
Institute for Ethnographie and Poklore
Praha 2, Lazarska 8, CSSR

Denmark

Dr. Klaus Ferdinand
Aarhus University
Aarhus, Denmark

H. Larsen
National Museet
Ny Vestergade 10
Kobenhavn, Denmark

Ecuador

P. Ernesto Alvarez A., Director
Centro misional de investigacionescientificas
Apartado 472
Quito, Ecuador

Egypt

Prof. M. Amer
8 rue Salamlek
Garden City, Le Caire
Republique Arabe vnie

Finland

Prof. Niilo Valonen
Ethnological U Institute
University of Helsinki
Fabianinkatu 33
Helsinki 17, Finland

France

Prof. J. Cuisenier
Musee des Arts et Traditions Populaires
Palais de Chailot
Paris 16e, France

Dr. Robert Gessain, Chairman
Committee on Ethnographic Museums
Musee de l'Homme
Place du Trocadero
Paris, France

Prof. Claude Levi-Strauss, Directeur
Le Laboratoire d'Anthropologie Sociale
College der France
11, Place Marcelin-Berthelot
Paris 3, France

Prof. Georges Olivier, Directeur
Laboratoire d'Anthropologie de la Faculte
des Sciences de Paris
Tours de Paris
11, quai Saint-Bernard,
75 Paris 5e, France

German Democratic Republic

Prof. Dr. Irmgard Sellnow
Deutsche Akademie der Wissenschaften zu Berlin
National komitee der DDR der anthropologischen
und ethnologischen Wissenschaften
108 Berlin, Democratic Republic of Germany

Federal Republic of Germany,

Prof. Dr. K. Jettmar, Stellvertreter
Sudasien-Institut der Universitat Heidelberg
SchaffelstraBe 6
Heidelberg, Federal Republic of Germany

Dr. Ilse von Schwidetzky, Direktor
Anthropolog sches Institut der
Johannes-Gutenberg-Universitat Mainz
Mainz, Federal Republic of Germany

Great Britain

Prof. Meyer Fortes
Department of Social Anthropology
Downing Street
Cambridge, CB2 3DZ, Great Britain

M. Christoph Furer-Haimendorf
School of Oriental and African Studies
University of London
London WC1, England

Dr. Geoffrey Ainsworth Harrison
Reader in Physical Anthropology
Fellow of Linacre College
Oxford, OX1 3BD, Great Britain

Greece

Dr. A.N. Poulianos
Hellenic Anthropological Association
7 Vissarionos Street
Athens 135, Greece

Guatemala

Calos Samayoa Chinchilla, Director
Instituto de Anthropologia e Historia
Edificio num. 5 de la Aurora Guatemala

Haiti

Dr. J.B. Romain
Faculte de Ethnologie
Universite d'Etat d'Haiti
10. Avenue Magloire Ambroise
Prot-au-Prince, Haiti

Honduras

Dr. Jesus Nunez Chinchilla, Directir
Instituto Nacianal de Antropologia e Historia de Honduras
Avenida Lempira No 404
Tegucialpa, Honduras, C.A.

Hungary

Dr. Tibor Bodrogi, Secretaire General
Magyar Neprajzi Tarsasag (Sicuete ethnographique hongroise)
Nonyves Ka 1 man—Korut 40 Budapest VIII
Hungary

Iceland

Prof. K. Eldjarn
Thjodminjasafn Islands
Reykjavik, Iceland

India

Prof. L.P. Vidyarthi
Department of Anthropology
Ranchi University
Ranchi/Bihar, India

Dr. Surajit C. Sinha
Department of Anthropology
University College of Science
35 Ballygunge Circular Road
Calcutta 19, India

Dr. B.N. Sahay
New Delhi

Dr. K.S. Mathur (Dr. P.K. Bhowmick)
Dr. D.P. Sinha
Indian Institute of Management
56a Barrakpore Trunk Road
Calcutta 50, India

Dr. Gopala Sarana
Dharwar

Dr. I.P. Singh
New Delhi

Iran

Prof. Ali Hanibal
Comite Iranien d' Anthropologie et d'Etnologie
Institut des Beaux Arts
Teheran

Ireland

Dr. A.T. Lucas
National Museum of Ireland
Kildare Street
Dublin 2, Ireland

Israel

Prof. Emanuel Marx
Department of Soziology and Anthropology
Tel Aviv University
Tel Aviv, Israel

Shlomo Deshen
Dept. of Soziology and Anthropology
Tel Aviv University
Tel Aviv, Israel

Harvey Goldberg
Dept. of Soziology and Anthropology
Hebrew University
Jerusalem, Israel

Phylis Palgi
Medical School,
Behavonal Science Department
Ministry of Health,
14, Arbaa Street
Tel Aviv, Israel

Henry Rosen Belt
Dept. of Anthropology and Soziology
Haifa University
Haifa, Israel

Patricia Smith
Dept. of Anatomy
Hebrew University
Jerusalem, Israel

Italy

Prof. Dr. Venerando Correnti, Direttore
Istituto die Antropologia "Giuseppe Sergi"
Universita di Roma
00185 Citta Universitaria
Rome, Italy

Prof. Enrico Cerulli
Italy

Prof. Giuseppe Genna
Italy

Prof. V.I. Grotanelli, Direttore
Istituto di Etnologia
Facolta di Lettere e Filosofia, citta Universitaria
Rome, Italy

Prof. Carlo Maxia
Italy

Prof. Raffaello Parenti
Italy

Ivory Coast

Dr. B. Holas
Centre des Sciences Humaines
B.P. 1600 Abidjan
(Rep. of) Ivory Coast

Japan

Prof. Chie Nakane
Organizing Committee of VIII CISAE
Science Council of Japan
Ueno Park, Tokyo
Japan

Prof. Dr. H. Suzuki,
Department of Anthropology
Faculty of Sciences
University of Tokyo
1 Motofuji-cho
Bunkyo-ku, Tokyo, Japan

Mexico

Dr. Ignacio Bernal, Director
Museo Nacional de Antropologia, Mexico
Bosque de Chapultepec, Mexcio 5, D.F.
Mexico

Prof. Dr. P. Bosch-Gimpera
Investigationes historicas, seccion de
Antropologia,
Torre de Humanidades, piso I
Ciudad Universitaria
Mexico 20 D.F.

Prof. Rubin de la Borbolla
Mexico

Prof. Dr. Juan Comas
Mexico

Prof. Dr. G. Bonfil
Director of the Instituto Nacional de Anthropologia,
Cordoba 45, Mexico.

Prof. Dr. J. Litwak
Section of Anthropology
Torre de Humanidades, piso I
Ciudad Universitaria
Mexico 20 D.F.

Monaco

L. Barrale, Conservateur
Musee d' Antropologie Prehistorique
Monaco (Principaute de Monaco)

Morocco

M. Henri Terrasse, Directeur
Institut des Hautes Etudes Marocaines,
Rabat

Netherlands

Dr P.E. DeJosselin De Jong
Department of Anthropology
University of Leiden
Netherlands

Prof. Dr. A.J.F. Kobben
University of Amsterdam
Amsterdam, Holland

Dr. H.J.M. Claessen
Institute of Cultural and Anthropology
Leiden University
Stationsplein 10,
Leiden, Netherlands

Dr. J. Huizinga
Institute of Anthropobiology
Utrecht University
Achter de Dom 22-24
Utrecht, Netherlands

New Zealand

Dr. Peter Gathercole, Senior Lecturer in Charge
Anthropology Department, University of Otago,
Dunedin

Nigeria

Allen Bassing, Curator
Jos Museum
Jos, Nigeria

Norway

Prof. Dr. Knut Kolsrud
Ethnological Institute
Universitetet l Oslo
Blindern
Oslo 3, Norway

Panama

Dr. Reina Torres de Arauz
Directora de Patrimonio Historico,
del Instituo Nacional de Cultura y
Deportes
Panama

Peru

E. Linares Malaga
Museo de Arqueologia e Historia
Universidad Nacional de San Agustin, calle
Nueva 414, Arequioa, Peru

Poland

Prof. Dr. Witold Hensel
Polska Akademia Nauk
Instytut Historii Kultury Materialnej
Warszawa, ul. Dluga 26
Poland

Prof. Dr. Witold Dynowski
Poland

Prof. Tadeusz Dzierzykray-Rogalski
ul. Kasprowicza 91
01-949 Warszawa,
Poland

Prof. Dr. K. Jazdzewski
Poland

Doc. Dr. Bronislaw, Jaworska
Poland

Prof. Dr. Halina lilicer
Poland

Romania

Dr. S. Milcu
Academia Republicii Populare Romine
Calea Vicotriei 12, Bucuresti
Romania

Prof. Olga C. Necraso
Laboratorul de Morfologie
Animala
Universitatea IASI
Romania

Prof. Mihai Pop, Director
Institutul de Etnografie si Folclor
Academia R.S.R.
Str. Nikos Beloiannis 25
Bucuresti 30696, Romania

Senegal

Th. Monod, Directeur
Charge du Departement de Linguistique, M. Houis
B.P. 205
Institut francais d'Afrique Noire, Dakar

Somalia

Dr. Yassin Osman Kenadid, Director
Cultural Relations
Ministry of Education
Mogadishu

Spain

Prof. Jose Manuel Gomez-Tabanera
Director del Departamento de Anthropologia y Etnologia
Universidad de Oviedo
Oviedo, Spain

Sweden

Prof. A. Hult Krant
Stockholms Hogskola, Drottninggatan 116
Stockholm, Sweden

Prof. Dr. K.G. Izikowitz
Etnografiska Museet
Norra Hamngatan 12
Goteborg, Sweden

Switzerland

Prof. Pierre Moeschler
Dept. d' Anthropologie
de L'universite de Geneve
12, rue Gustave—Revilliod
1227 Acacias—Geneve
Suisse

Dr. Gerhard Baer
Direktor des Museums f. Volkerkunde
Augustinerstr. 2
4000 Basel
Schweiz

Prof. J. Gabus
Musee d'Ethnographie
rue Saint—Nicholas 4
Neuchatel, Switzerland

Prof. Ernst-C. Buchi
Switzerland

Togo

Dr. F.N. Agblemagnon
Docteur en Sociologie
Centre d'Etudes Sociologiques
82, rue Cardinet
Paris XVII, France

Tunis

Centre national de recherches et d'Archeologie. Tunis
Ministere des Affaires culturelles. Tunis
c/o **Dr. Ali Sahly**, Rieumes (H.G.) (France)

Turkey

Prof. Dr. Nermin Erdentug, Director
Institute of Anthropological Sciences
Ankara University
Ankara, Turkey

Prof. Dr. Orhan Acipayamli
Ankara Unversitesi
Dil ve Tarih, Cografya Fakultesi
Sihhiye
Ankara, Turkey

Dr. Armagan Saatcioglu
Ankara Universitesi
Dil ve Tarih, Cografya Fakultesi
Sihhiye,
Ankara, Turkey

United States

Dr. Sol Tax
Department of Anthropology
University of Chicago
Chicago, Illinois, 60637, USA

Margaret Mead
15 W 77th St.
New York, N.Y. 10024, USA

Paul T. Baker
Department of Anthropology
Social Sciences Building
Pennsylvania State University
University Park, Pa. 16802, USA

William Irving
Department of Anthropology
University of Toronto
Toronto 5, on., Canada

Elizabeth Colson
Department of Anthropology
University of California
Berkeley, Ca. 94720, USA

Gabriel W. Lasker
31339 Pierce
Birmingham, Mi. 48009, USA

Uruguay

Instituto de Estudios Superiores
Constituyente 1711
Montevideo, Uruguay

USSR

Dr. Julian Bromley, Director
Moskva V-36
ul. Dimitri Ulyanov 19
Institut Etnografii Akademii Nauk USSR

Dr. V.P. Jakimov
Moskva K-9
Karl-Marx Prospekt 18
Institut Antropologii
Moskovskogo Universiteta
USSR

S.A. Arrontionnov
USSR

Ju. P. Averkieva
USSR

D.A. Olderogge
USSR

R.G. Kuzeev
USSR

Vatican

R.P.M. Schulien
Museo Missionario
Etnologico Palazzo Laterane
Piazza S—Giovanni in Laterane 6-A
Roma, Italy

Venezuela

Dr. Ramon Aveledo Hostos, Director-encargado
Museo de Ciencias Naturales. Caracas
Apartado 3893, Caracas

Yugoslavia

Prof. Dr. Milovan Gavazzi, President
Etnolosko Drustovo Jugoslavije (Societe ethnologique Yugoslave)
Studentski trg 13, p.f. 367
Beograd, Yugoslavia

Branimir Bratanic
Filozofski Fakultet,
Dure Salaja 3,
41001 Zagreb 2 (pp. 421)
Jugoslavija

Statutes of the IUAES

Art. 1. There shall be an International Union of Anthropological and Ethnological Sciences, hereinafter referred to as the Union. The present Statutes replace all former statutes as from the date of their formal approval by the Permanent Council.

Art. 2. (*a*) The Union is an international non-profit organization concerned with the advancement of knowledge.

(*b*) The Statutes of the Union are registered with the United Nations Educational Scientific and Cultural Organization, Paris, such registration constituting its act of incorporation.

(*c*) While not bound by the decisions or policies of the United Nations Educational Scientific and Cultural Organization, the Union may cooperate with and advise UNESCO.

Art. 3. The objectives of the Union are :

(*a*) To develop international scientific and professional cooperation (consistent with the Charter of UNESCO) in the fields of Anthropology and Ethnology, in the broadest sense in which these are understood in different parts of the world, and related disciplines and areas of study;

(*b*) To foster the development of scientific and professional institutions internationally and regionally;

(*c*) To stimulate scientific and professional cooperation

among institutions devoted to the relevant fields of knowledge;

(*d*) To cooperate with other international organizations, and particularly, though not exclusively, with the International Council for Philosophy and Humanistic Studies, the International Social Science Council, the International Council of Scientific Unions, International Association of Human Biologists and the International Council of Museums;

(*e*) To develop appropriate roles for anthropology and ethnology in international inter-disciplinary scientific endeavours;

(*f*) To take appropriate steps to meet any other objectives consistent with the international scientific and professional concerns of the membership, as determined by the Permanent Council and the Executive, and which are not inconsistent with Article 2(a) above.

Art. 4. The Union may affiliate with other organizations in a manner consistent with Articles 2 and 3, and may enter into contracts and establish committees, commissions and institutions to further its objectives.

Art. 5. There shall be the following categories of membership in the Union :

(*a*) National and internationally regional anthropological and/or ethnological societies and academies, recognized as such by the Executive Committee;

(*b*) Research institutions, university departments, and associations other than those defined in (a) above, which the Executive Committee deems are concerned with work in those disciplines referred to in Article 3(a);

(*c*) Individual members who shall be scholars active in research or teaching in those disciplines listed in Article 3(a), provided there is no regional or national organization in the country;

(*d*) Other organizations or institutions which, while not meeting the requirements of categories A or B, in the opinion of the Executive Committee contribute substantially to the work of the Union;

(*e*) Honorary Members, who shall be individuals appointed by the Permanent Council on the advice of the Executive Committee to a number not exceeding thirty. Honorary Members shall be selected on the grounds of outstanding contributions to scholarship, with due regard to a balance of regional and disciplinary representation. Honorary members shall not pay fees, and shall be appointed for life.

Art. 6. All applications for membership shall be directed to the Secretary-General of the Union. Decisions on membership status will be made by the Executive Committee, subject to appeal to the Permanent Council. The Executive Committee may appeal to the Permanent Council in the light of Article 5. The Executive Committee may delegate elements of its functions in respect of this article to a Membership Committee which the Executive Committee shall appoint.

Art. 7. Membership in the Union may be terminated :

(*a*) by resignation at any time;

(*b*) exclusion by the Permanent Council based on a two-thirds majority vote of delegations present for failure to comply with the conditions of Article 5;

(*c*) by failure to pay dues in accordance with the Statutes and the By-Laws, unless specifically exempted by the Executive Committee.

Art. 8. (*a*) There shall be a President of the Union, who shall also be President of the Congress.

(*b*) The President shall be appointed by the Permanent Council convened at the time of the International Congress of Anthropological and Ethnological Sciences upon the nomination of the national delegation of the country in which the next Congress shall take place.

(*c*) The President shall take office at the close of business of the Permanent Council sessions convened for the Congress at which the appointment is made.

(*d*) The President shall chair the Permanent Council, the General Assembly, and the Executive Committee, save that in case of inability to attend he shall designate an alternative chairman for that meeting only.

(*e*) The President shall not vote in the Permanent Council or the General Assembly unless otherwise provided for.

(*f*) Should the President cease to exercise his functions during his term, through death, illness or any other reason recognized by the Executive Committee, the Executive Committee shall appoint a successor for the remainder of the term from among the Vice-Presidents.

Art. 9. (*a*) There shall be seven Vice-Presidents who shall as far as practicable represent the variety of anthropological and ethnological disciplines and a balance of geographical representation.

(*b*) The Nominating Committee (Article 12) shall present nominations, with at least two names for each vacancy, to the Permanent Council for election.

(*c*) The Permanent Council shall elect three Vice-Presidents at one Congress and four at the next, in alternation, by majority of votes cast. In case of tied votes, the President shall have a casting vote.

Art. 10. (*a*) There shall be a Secretary-General of the Union who shall be appointed by the Permanent Council (for a five-year term) on the recommendation of the Executive Committee.

(*b*) The Secretary-General shall be the senior administrative officer of the Union and shall be responsible for the general oversight and administration of all activities under the authority of the Permanent Council, the President, the Executive, and other duly constituted committees.

(*c*) The Secretary-General of the Union shall not be responsible for the administration of the Congresses.

(*d*) The Secretary-General may receive salary on the decision of the Executive Committee.

(*e*) The Secretary-General shall maintain records of the affairs of the Union, minutes of General Assembly, Permanent Council and Executive Committee, statements of account; he shall maintain membership records; he shall administer the funds and property of the Union; he shall give notice of meetings.

(*f*) The Secretary-General shall appoint and manage the salaried staff of the Union.

Art. 11. (*a*) There shall be an Executive Committee which shall consist of the President, the immediate past President, the Vice-Presidents, and six additional members.

(*b*) The additional members shall be elected by the Permanent Council for terms of five years from the date of the immediately following Executive Committee meeting; save that if a Permanent Council meeting is not to be convened within one month of notice of vacancy being received by the Secretary-General, the Executive Committee may elect a member to fill such vacancy.

(*c*) The Executive Committee shall make policy decisions on behalf of and subject to the authority of the Permanent Council, shall appoint committees and delegate appropriate authority to them, shall authorize a budget, shall set membership fees, and shall authorize programmes of activity of an international scientific and professional nature, and shall take any other necessary steps on behalf of the Union, subject to the authority of the Permanent Council.

Art. 12. (*a*) There shall be a Nominating Committee appointed from time to time by the Executive Committee which will propose at least two candidates for every elective position referred to in Articles 8, 9, 10 and 11.

(*b*) The Nominating Committee shall make such other nominations as requested by the Executive Committee of the Permanent Council.

(*c*) For officers and other positions specifically referred to in the Statutes, additional nominations, may be made in accordance with such by-laws as the Permanent Council may from time to time approve.

Art. 13. (*a*) The governing body of the Union shall be the Permanent Council.

(*b*) The Permanent Council shall consist of national delegations and the Honorary Members.

(*c*) Each national delegation shall be entitled to one vote in decisions of the Council, and for purposes of voting each Honorary Member shall be considered to be an extra-numerary member of the national delegation of the country to which he is accredited.

(*d*) Each national delegation shall consist of up to six members, plus Honorary Members, who shall be appointed by the anthropologists and anthropological institutions of the country represented according to whatever procedure the anthropologists of that country determine.

(*e*) Only one delegation shall be accredited for any one country; in case of dispute as to which delegation shall be accredited, the Permanent Council shall elect an Accreditation Committee of three delegations to resolve the issue.

(*f*) National delegations shall register their names

and addresses with the Secretary-General, and shall designate their delegation Head.

(*g*) A quorum of the Permanent Council shall consist of one-fifth of the national delegations registered with the Secretary-General by the time of the commencement of the meeting.

(*h*) National delegations may delegate their rights to vote at a specified meeting to another national delegation, provided that such delegation be indicated in writing to the Secretary-General at least one month prior to the meeting, and provided that the national delegation named as the proxy agrees to serve in that capacity.

(*i*) The Permanent Council shall be convened at the International Congress, at least once in the interval between Congresses, and at any other time as determined by the President or the Executive Committee.

(*j*) The Permanent Council may act upon any matters concerning the Union or the Congress, subject to the Statutes.

(*k*) Unless otherwise determined by Statute or By-Law, all decisions of the Permanent Council shall be by majority of the national delegations present or represented by proxy. The President may exercise a casting vote in the event of a tie.

Art. 14. (*a*) There shall be a General Assembly of the Union which shall be advisory to the Permanent Council, the President and the Executive Committee.

(*b*) The General Assembly shall be convened at each Congress on the initiative of the President or the Secretary-General.

(*c*) The General Assembly shall consist of all members of the Union, without regard to category, in good financial standing.

(*d*) With regard to this Article, "good financial standing" shall mean that dues shall have been paid for the calendar year in which the meeting takes place, except that members who have been excused by the Executive Committee in pursuance of Articles 5(e) and 17 shall be considered also to be in "good financial standing".

(*e*) All members in whatever category shall be entitled to one vote.

(*f*) There shall be no proxy votes in the General Assembly.

(*g*) Resolutions of the General Assembly shall be adopted by majority vote of those present, and shall be referred to the appropriate organ of the Union for consideration and, where appropriate, action.

(*h*) The agenda for the General Assembly shall be circulated to national delegations in such a manner as could be reasonably expected to arrive at least one month prior to the date of the meeting, and shall be posted in a prominent position during the Congress.

(*i*) Items may be added to the agenda for the General Assembly by written request deposited with the Secretary-General at the Congress at least two days before the meeting, provided that such request be signed by at least ten members in good standing.

(*j*) The General Assembly may amend its own agenda by majority vote.

Art. 15. (*a*) There shall be periodic International Congresses of Anthropological and Ethnological Sciences which shall take place at intervals determined by the Permanent Council.

(*b*) At each Congress, the Permanent Council shall designate the time and place of the next Congress, for which the national delegation of the country in which the Congress is located shall form the Organizing Committee.

(*c*) The Organizing Committee for the Congress shall appoint a Secretary-General for the Congress, who shall be the principal administrative official of the Congress.

(*d*) The Organizing Committee shall appoint such other honorary, scientific and administrative committees as shall be deemed necessary, and shall have full authority over the theme, the finances, the administration, the locations within the country, invitations, communications, and all other matters pertinent to the operation of the Congress.

(*e*) The Organizing Committee shall present its overall plans for the Congress to the Permanent Council at least two years prior to the Congress, for discussion and advice.

(*f*) Participation in the Congress shall be open to bona fide anthropologists and ethnologists from any country.

(*g*) The Organizing Committee shall be responsible for the publication and language policy of the Congress.

Art. 16. (*a*) At the discretion of the Permanent Council, Inter-Congresses may be organized between Congresses at locations in countries which do not have the facilities or resources to take responsibility for World Congresses.

(*b*) The organization of Inter-Congresses shall be parallel to that for Congresses, with such modifications as the Permanent Council may approve from time to time to facilitate the task of the host delegation.

(*c*) In particular, the host delegation Organizing Committee may set limits upon the numbers of participants in the Inter-Congress and may select all or part of the participants by invitation or such other selective mechanism as approved by the Organizing Committee and the Permanent Council.

Art. 17. (*a*) The Executive Committee shall from time to time establish a scale of dues for each category of membership, and is authorized to waive or reduce the payment of dues in those instances in which it judges that financial or other considerations make payment onerous or impractical.

(*b*) Unless the Executive Committee has duly waived the payment of dues, members who have not paid their dues shall not have the right to vote.

Art. 18. (*a*) These Statutes hereby replace and amend any and all earlier Statutes of the Union as of the date of their adoption by the Permanent Council.

(*b*) Amendments to these Statutes may be made by a two-thirds majority of votes cast at a duly constituted meeting of the Permanent Council.

(*c*) Notice of amendment must be given to the Secretary-General nine months prior to the meeting of the Permanent Council at which the amendment is to be debated, and must be circulated to registered national delegations at least six months before that meeting.

(*d*) All matters and procedures not covered by the present Statutes shall be dealt with by the Executive Board, and reported to the Permanent Council.

(*e*) The Permanent Council may adopt by-laws to govern the operations of the Union insofar as these are not detailed by Statute.

(*f*) The Executive Committee shall appoint auditors and receive their reports.

(*g*) The President, the Secretary-General, and the Chairman of the Finance Committee may individually sign documents in the name of the Union relating to the receipts and disbursement of funds under their respective jurisdictions as from time to time determined by the Executive Committee, established in the Statutes, or set out in the By-Laws, and may each appoint a deputy to undertake this duty on his behalf when circumstances warrant.

(*h*) Any two of the President, the Secretary-General, the Chairman of the Finance Committee may sign contracts in the name of the Union other than those contracts referred to in paragraph (g) above;

provided that any one of the President, Secretary-General and Chairman of the Finance Committee plus any one member of the Executive Committee may also sign contracts.

(*i*) The Statutes are drawn originally in English and shall be translated into French. For interpretation purposes the original text in English shall be used. Languages of communication shall be French and English, and such other languages as used by UNESCO as are practicable. Languages of Congresses shall be English, French and such other languages as the national organizers determine.

By-Law No. 1

FINANCIAL DUES

The following schedule of annual dues shall be effected in and after 1979.

Art. 5 :

Category A. At a rate of 50 cents per bona fide professional anthropological or ethnological scholar who is a national, as distinct from foreign, member of the institution, as declared and defined by that institution, with a minimum of $25.00.

Category B. $25.00 in year of accession and in the year of the World Congress (of which $15.00 will be transmitted to the Congress); in other years $10.00.

Category C. $3.00.

Category D. As recognized in individual cases by the Executive Committee, provided that it is not less than $50.00 or twice that which would be charged if the institutions were eligible for membership under Category A.

Collection shall be by the Chairman of the Finance Comittee who shall maintain lists of paid-up members and report these to the Secretary-General.

The Chairman of the Finance Committee may authorize payment in other currencies under suitable terms and conditions, may operate bank accounts in the name of the Union, and may authorize the disposition of funds subject to the authority of the Executive.

Index